SEX, LIES, AND YOUR FUTURE

D1201075

Reverend Michael O'Connor

Sources cited upon request

POD Apostle Publishing
223 White Avenue
Ocean Springs, Mississippi 39564

Library of Congress Control Number 2014912200
ISBN 978-0-9887611-0-0

First Edition

Nihil obstat: †Monsignor T. Dominick Fullam, VG
Imprimatur: †Monsignor T. Dominick Fullam, VG

Cover Design
Reverend Michael O'Connor

Internal Design & Typesetting
Pam Bozeman

With Special Thanks
to Pam Bozeman for her invaluable help in
editing and organizing this manuscript;
to Mary Johnson for her assistance in editing; and to
Karen Renz for her artistic contributions.

Sex, Lies, and Your Future may be purchased in bulk for
educational, business, or fund-raising use. For ordering
information email: mpo39520@gmail.com.
Printed in the United States of America

For my parents, Ed & Marian O'Connor,
and parents everywhere

Prologue

How can you and I be happy today? What has gone wrong with the world? Why are so many people stressed, depressed, obese, numbing or cutting themselves, and hooked on drugs (prescription and otherwise)? This book examines how your actions and your family's actions impact your world, values, goals, and happiness. Furthermore, it seeks to answer why "the family" is the way it is today.

I believe many of these troubles are connected to sex, lies, and a misguided quest for happiness. The family as the cornerstone of our culture is in trouble, and when the family suffers, everyone suffers. Hopefully, you recognize the entire human race as your very extended family.

So what are some problems in "our American family"?

- Infidelity occurs in more than 40% of marriages.
- First marriages end in divorce at a rate of 40-50% (the rate is even higher for subsequent marriages).
- About 41% of babies are born to parents who are not married in the first place.
- 20-30% of girls and about 5% of boys experience sexual abuse by age 18. These numbers represent millions of damaged lives.
- We have a growing population of people who are addicted to pornography.
- A middle school principal recently informed me that they have *more than one* child at her school considered to be a sexual predator due to actions toward younger, smaller children.
- Not long ago, a parent spoke to me about a seven-year-old son having been sodomized by his nine-year-old neighbor. The nine-year-old had been in trouble

before because of sexual activity and, according to the parent who visited me, watches whatever he wants on the internet.

- Recently, a concerned mother told me some difficult news about her fifty-year-old daughter. This daughter is a twice divorced mother with her own adult children. She was abused by one husband and cheated on by the other. The concerned mother explained that the daughter had given up on men and decided to try life as a lesbian and is currently living with her girlfriend. Furthermore, one of her children has followed mom's lead and is also living as a lesbian.

I could go on and on and on. These people are all of our mothers, fathers, sons, daughters, children, teachers, students, neighbors, and friends. It could be you. I wish these were isolated incidences within the human family, but they are frighteningly common.

It is a challenge to present the Christian message about sex and family in a positive way, particularly in the sound-bite, text-message generation in which we live. Admittedly, some of the "thou shall not" sayings seem restrictive and boring. But I know now, "Thou shall not commit adultery" is a message of love and a timeless commandment given by a Father *who loves His children*. I do not think it an accident that it is short and easy to memorize. Our Father who gave us life truly knows what we need.

Today, people want the why and not just the commandments. I hope in reading this book that you find "the why" and that God, your Creator and Father, really does know what is best for His children and their happiness, even when the path to happiness is narrow and challenging.

The call to sexual purity outside of marriage and truly holy sex within marriage will sound, at least on the surface, like "don't drink" to a thirsting man floating on a lake; but the sexual waters from which most people are trying to drink is salt water and is making them thirstier, and this water, no matter how well packaged, will never satisfy the thirsty soul.

Reverend Michael O'Connor

Contents

A Physician's Perspective

Virginity, Chastity, Abstinence, Marriage...

Do these things really matter?

Well, that is a question I have asked not only myself but also the high school seniors at our local Catholic high schools. As a Catholic, married, mother of five, who also happens to be an OBGYN, I have dealt with these issues in many different contexts over my lifetime. My answer to these questions would have been different at different points in my maturity. Now, I can unequivocally answer that yes, these issues matter a lot and these issues affect a lot of different arenas of life. I try to pass on to the students a little of my experience to encourage them to think for themselves about these issues so that they don't blindly follow the culture, like so many people do.

Like many others, both Catholic and non-Catholic, I spent much effort denying God's laws that are impregnated in my heart. These truths are solidified at our baptism and help us form our conscience. It wasn't until well into adulthood and after 12 years of practicing medicine that I finally took the time to educate myself about the Catholic teachings on sexuality, reproduction, contraception, and marriage. I read the papal teachings by John Paul II concerning contraception; I studied *Humanae Vitae* and *Redemptoris Mater* with a local Endow group. I also attended non-denominational Bible Studies for women. All of these experiences have brought me more perspective and understanding. They have also convinced me that the Catholic Church has the TRUTH. It is not an easy truth to accept in this cultural climate.

I spent much of my Catholic upbringing sort of deaf, dumb, and blind to what was being taught and spoken about in church. I am a cradle Catholic, but I did not have a strong religious background. Although I attended an all-girl Catholic High School in New Orleans, Louisiana, I did not see that these teachings had much direct impact on my life. God was in me and I definitely believed in Him but I was not concerned with details. Somehow, I always thought He wanted more for me and from me, but I chose to ignore a lot of His directions. As my life grew, things didn't make sense anymore and eventually I could see how much of a mess I was making of it. I could also see how much of a mess our society was making of this world. Knowing the family is the foundation of all communities, I recognized that the utter disregard we were giving to the sanctity of sexuality and human relationships was dissolving the very foundations on which we were supposed to stand.

I also realized that these issues do not "go away" once you are married. Once a couple is married it would seem that issues related to procreation and contraception would be easier to handle. For the vast majority of couples it does not seem to get easier. The exception to that, in my opinion, would be the couples whom I observed practicing Natural Family Planning. When a couple has consciously chosen to work together on these issues, it seems that they function with two basic ground rules. One, all human life is considered a welcome blessing. And two, sexual activity is NEVER without a responsibility to care for their spouse physically, emotionally, and sexually.

A few examples of how these issues continue to present themselves even after marriage come to mind.

Many years ago I had a patient present to my office in her early forties complaining of hot flashes and insomnia, just generally not feeling well. She had been having irregular menstrual cycles and felt she was entering early stages of menopause. She was an attractive, physically fit woman who had been married for about twenty years and had never had children. She and her husband had gone through extensive fertility treatments without success. Her husband was in his fifties and they seemed to be sharing their lives well. During that visit we discovered that she was pregnant! It was so exciting!! She was shocked and ecstatic. We drew her prenatal labs, started her on vitamins, and talked about pregnancy. We exchanged many hugs, and as I watched her walk down the hall to schedule her initial OB visit she seemed to be levitating with joy. It was so wonderful to be a part of that moment with her.

A few weeks passed and she did not return to see me. This would happen at times for a variety of reasons. Sometimes it was financial or due to insurance coverage, and sometimes a patient would just choose another doctor. Whatever the reason, I thought of her from time to time and would smile and wish her well.

A couple of months later this patient returned and was complaining again of not sleeping, hot sweats, and other peri-menopausal symptoms. She did not look well. I learned that she had gone home with her exciting news and found that her husband was not "ready" to be a parent at this point in his life.

In his opinion it was no longer a good time for them to have a baby. Ultimately, they decided to abort the baby. I believe that if they had been committed to an openness to life this tragic situation would have been avoided.

Another patient of mine presented asking for an abortion. Her demeanor begged for a discussion. She did not look like she wanted to ask for the procedure. As I explained that I did not perform pregnancy terminations, I learned what led her to ask for an abortion. She was a married mother of two teenagers and she had been having an adulterous affair. Her husband had had a vasectomy. She discovered that she was pregnant and was now faced with having to tell her husband about the affair and pregnancy, and explaining to her children why she was having a baby after so many years. I do not know the outcome of that situation, but I know it was painful.

With the comfort of her husband's vasectomy this patient had not worried about conceiving in the marital bedroom. One responsibility of lovemaking had been distanced from its pleasure. Once again I found myself reflecting on this woman's situation and I believe it could very likely destroy her marriage and the relationships she shared with her children. Adolescents can be incredibly hard on a parent who does something so obviously wrong. Life is often very black and white at that age and only with time can a child understand a parent and his or her humanness.

When both partners share the responsibilities related to sexuality it requires communication, negotiation, and commitment. It is far from easy. I see this as a truth that covers premarital relationships and marital relationships.

Prior to marriage, sexual activity is associated with basically nothing good. Its consequences can be pregnancy, sexually transmitted infections, shame, depression, eating disorders, and a warped sense of what relationships are supposed to be. Relationships should be entered into freely, and they are designed to bring out the strengths in each partner. I believe that any parent can guess when a child is too physically involved with their girlfriend or boyfriend. They start bickering. There is drama. It is not an absolute indicator, but it certainly sends up a flag. One or the other person is too dependent on the relationship and things that shouldn't be an issue become points of contention. "He wants to go hunting." "She was flirting with some guy at the mall." "He has to go to his grandmother's birthday party instead of spending the evening with me." "Her parents came home unexpectedly." "She has to study." "He has basketball practice." Well, I'd say that all of those examples can get blown out of proportion when one person or the other is overly involved with a premarital relationship. Young men should go hunting and attend their grandmothers' birthday parties and play basketball. Young women should talk to other males and study, and it should not matter when their parents come home to their own house!!!

I challenge high school seniors to look at their greatest achievements—athletic or academic—and ask them if it is easy to place first at state or receive the National Merit Scholarship. Of course, the answer is no. But then I ask them if it was worth the effort. They unanimously say, "YES." I assure them that while these Catholic teachings are hard to achieve they will reap the reward with their spouse.

Virginity, Chastity, Abstinence, Marriage...yes, they matter. They not only matter now, they matter for eternity. This book will help you to understand why.

Michele Pisciotta, M.D.

SEX, LIES, AND YOUR FUTURE

1

Sex, Lies, and Your Future

You want to be happy. No sane person needs to be convinced of the desire for happiness. Your right to seek happiness, derived from being created in God's image, is enshrined in our Declaration of Independence:

> We hold these Truths to be self-evident, that all Men are created equal, that they are endowed by their Creator with certain unalienable Rights, that among these are Life, Liberty, and the pursuit of Happiness.

How do You Pursue Happiness?

I once served as a volunteer waiter at a large dinner party where the wine was free and the food was late, very late. One of my fellow waiters reported to the kitchen concerning his table, "They are drunk, and they are not happy!" And they probably weren't. I can imagine that after many of those partygoers had eaten and been, for a time, "happy," they awakened the next morning— predictably less than happy once again. The pursuit of happiness is a little more challenging than requesting it from your waiter, mate, pharmacist, jester, parent, phone, or television. "I'm bored... make me happy."

It is often the case that happiness may be a great struggle for many because of the circumstances of one's family. I once had a wise mother tell me, "The most important relationship children will ever have is the relationship between their parents." Remember, *no sane person needs to be convinced that he or she wants to be happy*. And no sane person needs to be convinced of the desire for one's children to be happy.

You have the *responsibility* to be happy.

However, you might need encouragement to believe that happiness is tied to the pursuit of virtue, a purpose, goodness, and self-control; one might also need to be convinced that happiness comes from within.

You have the *responsibility* to be happy. For this book to make any sense we must agree first that you want to be happy; and second, that happiness does not wholly depend on immediate and/or external circumstances.

What are You? Who are You?

What is human nature? Human nature answers the question, "What are you?" Answered correctly, you are a beloved child, a child of God created by Him, in His image and likeness. As God's life was breathed into the "dust" (matter), your nature was created. You are body *and* spirit; rather, bodyandspirit together—incomplete without both, separated only at death.

You are *not* an accident at the end of a long string of accidents. You are much more than a collection of proteins. What are you? You are precious, lovable, loved by God, and capable of knowing you are loved and of giving love in return. Because of the nature of your human spiritual soul, you are called to and perfected by love.

Who are you? You are attracted by the true, the good, and the beautiful. You and I are beings who see, know, think, love, and choose; *but*—and this is crucial—we see dimly, know in part, think with distraction, love with a degree of selfishness, and, at times, choose wrongly. Furthermore, we do evil things; sometimes, even when we wish not to, we do evil. We fall off the wagon and throw others under the bus. That is our nature. Human nature, as we experience it, is *fallen*, and that which is true, good, and beautiful becomes distorted in our pursuits and perceptions. Pursuing the whims of our fallen nature does not lead to happiness. In other words, you (and I) are not always so good at pursuing happiness. As an old country song once suggested, we are often looking for love in all the wrong places.

Dear reader, I invite you to consider this proposition: Something is fundamentally "wrong" with your nature...with you. You are often not at your best. This is not meant to be an insult or condemnation—it is a fact that applies to you and, in varying degrees, to everyone else on the planet. The good news is that you can and should experience healing, and then mature to greater and greater spiritual, moral, and emotional health, i.e., happiness.

Sick nature is not healed by denial, changing the law, or altering the *Diagnostic and Statistical Manual of Mental Disorders.*

(Used by psychologists and others, this handbook is a commonly accepted guideline for describing or categorizing disorders in human thought and behavior.) Corrupted human nature is not successfully treated by "self-esteem" programs and empty praise designed to make people believe, "I'm OK!" Human nature *needs* to be healed. More than healed, it needs to be remade, redirected, "reborn" if you will; not simply soothed, numbed, and distracted by "sex, drugs, rock and roll," power, praise, prestige, crunchy-salty-sweet snacks, liposuction, Botox, "retail therapy," antidepressants, sports, alcohol, or tobacco. Though not necessarily evil things in themselves, when these become the purpose of life and the focus of happiness they will, in time, fail, lie, and lead astray.

Jesus calls the happiness this book points toward "blessedness." Blessedness survives all attacks but requires spiritual health. It is true and lasting. At times, blessedness is far removed from present physical or emotional circumstances, and it does not simply happen by chance. Rather, it must be pursued, and is often found in places one would never look without grace, the help of heaven.

Sex and Happiness

Some years ago I listened to a talk on sex and various related issues by Janet Smith, Ph.D., titled, "Contraception: Why Not." Assuming that the goal of our pursuits is happiness for ourselves, friends, and children, Dr. Smith, a Catholic philosopher and theologian, began with the claim that if modern people had to choose from among going forward in life without their car, computer, or contraception, they would have a very difficult choice before them. She argued that contraception, which literally means "against the beginning" (in this case against the beginning of life), and contraception's allowance of casual sex was seen as a necessary part of modern life and happiness, or at least of the pursuit of happiness.

Around the time I first heard her talk, I believed, perhaps as you do now, that sexual morality, and particularly contraception's role in sexual morality, was a minor teaching of the Catholic Church, and in fact something the Catholic Church was wrong about. I believed one could be a "good" Catholic, a good Christian, believe in one's heart, and profess with one's lips that "Jesus is Lord" while simultaneously, *willfully* rejecting (what I would later come to learn is) the clear, historical, and timeless Christian teaching on sexual morality. This I believed because of my [*mis*]understanding and experience of human progress. I now know I believed and perpetuated lies in both my speech and actions.

2

Sin: More Than a Bad Choice

Contrary to popular belief and modern marketing, sin is not something fun, delicious, or exciting that God, the Bible, the Church, or the Surgeon General have arbitrarily ruled against. Rather, to sin is to miss the mark: to fail to see, pursue, or strive for the goal of human life which is to know and to love, Love. To sin is to wander off the way, to get lost. Ben Franklin said that sin is not hurtful because it is forbidden, it is forbidden because it is hurtful. A sin is an offense against God, love, truth, reason, and right conscience. Sin destroys. Sin is a sickness of the soul and a cause of further sickness. A saint once said that sin is an abuse of the God-given power to do good. Sin is a form of insanity where insanity is the refusal or incapacity to know right from wrong, good from evil, reality from falsehood, what is hurtful from what is helpful. As we will see, this kind of "insanity" can be quite rationally embraced when grace is rejected.

Sin may be fun, but whether we can see it or not, sin is

fun in the same way vacationing on the payroll and "stiffing" your employees is fun. Sin is refreshing the way sleeping in and missing "the big final exam" is refreshing. Sin often scratches the immediate itch of a disordered human nature through indulging laziness, lust, gluttony, pride, vanity, anger,

Sin is an abuse of the God-given power to do good.

cowardice, etc. Sin may really feel good for a time—even for a long time—or provide an escape from some difficulty; but scratching the itch doesn't heal the wound, love does. All sin works against the good of the individual and the human family. Much more on this later, but please hear this clearly: Jesus Christ did not come to condemn you for being a sinner or for being inclined to sin, which you certainly are, or for being in the darkness of ignorance. Jesus came to save sinners, seek the lost, and light the darkness. God wills that all people be saved *and* come to knowledge of the truth. Sin goes against God's will. God permits us to sin if we choose.

> *"Amazing Grace, how sweet the sound, that saved a wretch like me. I once was lost but now am found, was blind, but now, I see."*
> *- John Newton*

An Analogy: Junk Sex

Consider a more visible and tangible problem akin to the often invisible and perhaps disbelieved problem of sexual sin. Eating is required for human sustenance and can be a great pleasure and joy. Eating can be so much more than refueling;

it is a way of family sharing, deal making, celebrating, communion, and fellowship. With all due respect to those who are genetically predisposed to obesity and acknowledging that we must contend with slick marketing, sedentary jobs, and processed and junk food, for most people the first and often only cause of obesity is giving in to the desire to eat too much. This desire is rooted in a "disordered" attraction to the pleasure or relief brought about by eating. In human beings, this disorder should be controlled and transformed by our will, sense of purpose, and self-discipline.

Of course there is "fun" on the way to obesity, but the destination can include damaged health, a kind of disfigurement, pain, reduced mobility, depression, dependence, diabetes...all problems for both the individual and for society. As the number of obese Americans continues to rise, as do individuals with other eating disorders (anorexia, bulimia, etc.), I contend that the number suffering *far worse* in their minds and souls from the often-invisible disorder—sin—of lust is *much* higher.

Furthermore, giving in to an unhealthy craving for food or undisciplined sexual impulses does not make it go away. Giving in only puts it on hold and perpetuates a cycle. Soon, the urge will call again and ring and ring and ring and ring. Whether you are lean or large, the power of vice and fallen nature should *not* control your values and behavior; rather, discipline, virtue, grace, and sanity should lead us all to disconnect from that incessant ringing and live a life of self-control and happiness on earth, and eternal beatitude with God in heaven.

So, just as we suffer individually and collectively from *junk food*, we suffer from *junk sex* and a distorted understanding of our bodies and spirits. The analogy is imperfect, and not every disorder begins as a sin, but it points our understanding in the right direction.

Works of the Flesh and Fruits of the Spirit

I believe that the greatest fears of the human heart are of hunger, loneliness, and abandonment. So often, sin is in fact a misguided attempt at nourishment or communion of some kind. Jesus did not come to condemn human beings who happen to feel empty, lonely, or afraid—those grasping for satisfaction, love, and communion. It is no accident that perhaps the most powerful, personal, and initially public act of forgiveness in the Bible is of Jesus and the woman caught in "the very act of adultery." She is publicly ridiculed, rejected, and shamed. Jesus comes to forgive her, you, and me, and to offer us eternal communion with God. Jesus challenges the woman's accusers to throw stones only if they have no sins themselves and they leave, one by one, beginning with the oldest people gathered until eventually no one is left to condemn her. Jesus asks her, "Has no one condemned you?" She replies, "No one, Lord." He responds, "Neither do I condemn you, go and from now on sin no more" (John 8:1-11). In other words, Jesus tells us all: I did not come to condemn you, but quit committing adultery (i.e., sin)! Jesus knew this woman and He knows you. Unless you are insane, you want to be happy here and now, as well as in the future—forever. You want love, joy, peace, and patience.

The fruit of the Holy Spirit is offered to those in communion with God. Any farmer, any gardener, anyone with eyes to see knows that it takes time for fruit to grow. The "fruit of the Holy Spirit" includes love, joy, peace, patience (in suffering), kindness, goodness, faithfulness, gentleness, and self-control. Please note that the fruit of the Spirit is not simply the result of human labor—and it takes time to grow.

St. Paul contrasted these fruits with the behavior he called the "works of the flesh": sexual immorality, impurity,

> # Jesus did not come to condemn human beings who happen to feel empty, lonely, or afraid.

sensuality, idolatry, sorcery, enmity, strife, jealousy, fits of anger, rivalries, dissension, division, envy, drunkenness, orgies, and the like. These works flow all too easily from a human heart unaided by grace. Sure, *you can settle* for sexual immorality and/or drunkenness if you choose, but the fruit of the Spirit does not grow well in that soil (see Galatians 5:16-24).

The Search for Happiness

There is in man an eternal longing. The flesh may deny this longing but it cannot satisfy it. Sin often masks or hides this eternal longing. In the book, *The Search for Happiness*, the author,

Father Oscar Lukefahr, C.M., presents four levels of happiness. Each of these kinds of happiness is one part of the authentic joy of life.

The first is **pleasure**, which is rooted in food, drink, sex, etc. Father Lukefahr notes that this kind of "happiness" lasts only minutes, hours, or days until the biological urge is reset. The second kind of happiness he considers is that of **accomplishment**. This is the promotion, honor roll, trophy, the run completed, or race won. This happiness can be longer lasting—even to having an effect on a life for months or years. But eventually the next semester, sports season, or season of life begins. The third level of happiness is **relationships**: love, friendship, and the respect of others. This source of happiness can be deeply satisfying and span for decades, but these relationships fail to *fully* satisfy the maturing heart of man. Even the very best of love relationships are ultimately threatened by at least one of these: death, disease, drift, and betrayal. Finally, there is the fourth level of happiness: our eternal union, our **communion** with God and each other (the

> # The more one gives into temptation (sins) and wanders off the way, the stronger will be the desire to believe that the lie is true and the truth is false.

Communion of Saints), which begins now. This communion is lived in faith, hope, and love—the virtues poured into us by grace.

Again, none of the first three levels of happiness are bad in themselves, but when the higher is traded for the lower a corner is turned, and we steer away from our purpose and "miss the mark"; we sin. Sin is a lie. Sin is death. The very nature of sin is that it is "tempting and attractive." But sin is false. The more one gives into temptation (sins) and wanders off the way, the stronger will be the desire to believe that the lie is true and the truth is false.

Sins of the Flesh: Sins of the Spirit

The woman mentioned above, "caught in the very act of adultery," was certainly guilty of a sin, a sin of the flesh. The sins of the flesh are serious, and they are nearly universal; everyone, in one way or another, has been or will be guilty of a sin of the flesh. This book deals mostly with sins of the flesh, but not because these are the worst of all sins; no, because they are the most common temptations, especially so for the young. The worst of sins, which blind our eyes and harden our hearts, are the sins of the spirit: pride and disobedience. When one rejects the truth that the sins of the flesh are truly sins, it is comparable to the woman caught in adultery telling Jesus, who came not to condemn her, but to save her, "I don't need you or your forgiveness." This easily transitions to, "If this 'Jesus Savior' thinks what I am doing is a sin, then I positively reject Him, and His unsought forgiveness."

The initial stage of an adult life in the Spirit is overcoming the most fundamental sins: lust (sexual sins), gluttony (other pleasures of the flesh including excesses in food, alcohol, and drugs), and so on. Many people spend much of their spiritual lives stuck in the first stage, struggling to grow to the next phase of the spiritual life, some perhaps because they don't take these sins of the flesh seriously enough. Today, however, more and more people mired in these sins are tempted to reject the idea that there is sin being committed at all. When this happens, one becomes immediately susceptible to pride and its deadly powers of blindness and self-righteousness.

Sins of the flesh are not the worst of sins, but unforgiven, unhealed, and unchanged they morph into sins of the spirit. I challenge and invite you to exercise your critical thinking while being open to the truth—no matter where it leads. This book is about sex, lies, and the future, but it is also about love and happiness—your happiness—in life and in eternity.

3

Sex, Contraception, and the Recent Past

Did you know that in 1925 Mahatma Gandhi made the prophetic statement, "I urge the advocates of artificial methods [of birth control] to consider the consequences. Any large use is likely to result in the dissolution of the marriage bond"? In other words, he predicted that contraception would destroy families. Again, Gandhi told his followers: "There is hope for a decent life only so long as the sexual act is definitely related to the conception of precious life."

At the time when Gandhi—a Hindu, pacifist, and peace activist—made these statements, there was a near universal consensus in Christian teaching. Every single major Christian group would have agreed with him on this principle. The biggest names in the history of Protestant theology—John Calvin, Martin Luther, John Wesley and many others—clearly and scripturally taught the reality that contraception is a sin. By the 1960s, less than two generations after Gandhi made these statements, the only major Christian group in the world that would agree with the wise old Hindu about contraception was the Catholic Church. (Notably, Amish Christians and the Mormons also reject contraception, as well as a very few but growing number of scattered Protestant Congregationalists.)

Are you aware of what the atheist and father of psychiatry, Sigmund Freud, said in regard to contraception? Freud said the criterion by which one judges whether a sexual activity is perverse is if it departs from being open to life and pursues the attainment of gratification independently. Moreover, he believed that contraception undermined both self-control and self-discipline, and when these fundamentals of health were weakened, a path to neurosis was opened in the mind. Neurosis is mental distress and anxiety...an invisible mental injury. One psychologist described neurosis as looking at the world and oneself in a way distorted by compulsive needs, rather than reality. This "invisible injury" is incredibly common in the modern world. More common even than obesity, I suspect.

In the history of this country, lawmakers—most of whom were Protestant—have passed laws against the sale or distribution of contraceptives. Why would they have done this? Were they ignorant misogynists (woman-haters) who did not like sex? No. History shows they did this because they believed that vice, in the form of sexual immorality and lust, would spread in the wake of artificial contraception. They believed that sexual immorality would weaken the family and society in general, that contraception and sexual immorality violated natural law, and that contraception was contrary to the teachings of Sacred Scripture.

I believe that often the less that is "illegal," the better. My intent is not to address the legality of contraception. On the other hand, laws clearly teach the values of a society, and the "law of the land" *must* rest on some *ultimate* conviction, a foundation stone. The fact is that all of these voices were in agreement with the timeless and current Catholic teaching. But today the Catholic Church is something like a lone voice in the desert.

A Step along the Way to Where the World is Today in Sexual Morality

In 1930, leaders of the Church of England decided by vote to change a moral evil into a moral good. After a number of failed attempts, they embraced artificial contraception within marriage and under certain circumstances. With their newfound "knowledge of good and evil," these churchmen convinced themselves and much of the world that contraception was good, and had a string of practical reasons and proposed benefits that would flow from their hope and change.

For perhaps the first time in Christianity, what had been taught for 1,900 years as the "sin of Onan" (see Genesis 38) was now officially embraced as something good. Within a short time, every major Protestant group, devoid of Tradition, followed in the steps of the Anglicans. Tradition here is understood as what the Church, in union with Sacred Scripture, has always and universally held to be true. (Onan is a person in the Old Testament who spilled his semen [sperm, seed] on the ground rather than fathering a child.)

So what was the Catholic Church's response to the Church of England's vote? Pope Pius XI wrote a letter titled *Casti Connubii* (*On Christian Marriage*). In it he affirmed that sex is holy and life-giving by its *nature*. Furthermore, the Pope tried to expose what he called "false principles of a new and utterly perverse morality" that would poison the world. He reiterated that children are a blessing to marriage and that parents have the personal right and the personal duty to educate their children. He said prophetically that true Christian marriage was under attack. This was in 1930! Almost 100 years ago, Pope Pius XI saw that there were greater issues at stake than what met the eye: issues like the integrity of the family, the meaning of sex, the purpose of marriage, the place of children within a family, and the sanctity of life itself.

From the 1930s to the 1960s there was little debate on the subject in Catholicism. Many Catholics, in fact the majority, continued to believe and follow the teaching of the Church in regard to birth control. They were obedient, and obedience—a virtue that led Jesus to carry His cross—was then considered something good and necessary in Christianity. By the end of the 1960s, however, law, religion, and society had embraced contraception nearly universally. Soon, the law, religion, and society would have to allow for failed contraception and embrace abortion. But I am getting ahead of myself.

4

The Polarization

On one hand, artificial contraception and sterilization are thought of as great advances for civilization: a "miracle pill" and effective solutions to the so-called normal, but actually disordered, sexual appetites that infect human nature. These solutions are thought necessary in today's world to attain happiness as well as for the stewardship of the earth. This is the ideology of much of the world, from professed Christians to the Communist Chinese.

On the other hand, the Catholic Church teaches that the pursuit of sterile sex by using contraceptive products and behaviors, abortion, sterilization, and same-sex acting out has had horrendous consequences for individuals, families, and society. Additionally, it has made many (particularly the young) generally less virtuous, less disciplined, less happy, less Christian, less loving, and more confused about the nature and purpose of their bodies and lives.

The Miracle Pill

"Life is difficult." Never has a truer statement been

written. Even happy lives include suffering, for suffering is inevitable. This truth is not limited to a Christian worldview. Buddha said, "Life is suffering." Nietzsche said, "To live is to suffer; to survive is to find some meaning in the suffering."

So why did so people many embrace artificial contraception? Obviously, the answer is to ease suffering: for an easier life, a better life, for better "love." The industrial revolution, medical revolution, technological revolution, and the resulting urban and suburbanization rapidly introduced society to advances that promised, and in many ways really delivered, a better life. Meanwhile, the power of modern marketing began to package consumerism (buy this, eat those, experience that and be happy) with materialism (have the latest stuff and be happy). These campaigns framed a picture of life where children were not really a blessing but rather part blessing, part environmental hazard, part expense, and oftentimes obstacles to happiness—especially women's happiness. Simply put, more of society embraced individualism and its philosophy of "It's all about me, and if you are a part of that, OK, *but it is still all about me.*"

At some point there began a renewed and sustained push for better birth control. This push had both a technological and philosophical backing. In the 1960s, development of a new type of contraception emerged: "The Pill." This pill was different from all other pills. It was <u>THE</u> Pill and it was literally claimed to be a *miracle* drug. People *celebrated* that so many of life's difficulties and unhappy circumstances were on the cusp of being solved by the Pill. Suffering, abortion, divorce, abuse, poverty, ghettos, crime, addiction, sprawl, pollution, and maybe even neurosis...the Pill promised hope and change, a **solution** to these, once and for all.

"Miraculously," the Pill, as the solution to some of individuals' and society's greatest problems, _did not_ call for self-discipline, patience, or self-control but promised pleasure, license, and freedom from responsibility. Some "theologians" hailed the pill as a gift from God. What was not to like about it? The following list is typical of what has been described as the promised benefits of cheaper, better, and more widely available contraception.

- Divorce would go away; marriage and families would be strengthened.
  - Most stress would be eliminated from marriage, making sex within marriage much better and therefore marriages much better.
  - Previously, husbands were stressed out over too many children, budget problems, and financial worries; fewer children and working moms would mean less stress and more "stuff," leading to happier lives and healthier marriages.
  - Free from the fear of pregnancy, young couples could "test drive" one another sexually and choose "the right model."
  - Rather than getting married out of desperation for sex, one could now wait patiently and find the perfect (properly test-driven) partner.
- More choices would make for more happiness for women.
- Women would now really be the equivalent of men; many of their problems would simply disappear and they could have sex and not get pregnant.
- The end of poverty was at hand because there would be no large families and very, very few single mothers—and most of those few would be by choice.

- With the end of poverty there would be reduced crime, fewer people in jail, and less drug abuse.
- Domestic and national security would even mean fewer problems between nations.
- Every child would be planned and wanted.
  - No abortions
  - No unwanted children or foster children
  - The end of fatherlessness

As the promises of the Pill really began to be marketed, I am told there was a tangible expectation of the coming happiness and freedom stemming from a cultural and sexual revolution. Some of these hoped-for benefits were "reasonable" according to human wisdom and it was believed they would all come to pass very quickly. But they have *mostly not materialized* because human nature and natural law (God's wisdom) have been overlooked. Advocates today are still promising a full flowering of these benefits if only we have more, better contraception (and/or abortion) provided "free" (that is to say, at taxpayer expense but without taxpayer assent) and without parental consent, including to children beginning in middle school or even earlier. But as we will see, while the arguments may be convincing, they are full of errors and lies.

One has to give oneself away in order to love, and one cannot give that which one does not possess.

What's Love Got to Do with It

Believe it or not, Christianity teaches that lasting human happiness (even in this short life) is not rooted in pleasures or possessions. Happiness is rooted in love, love that heals. Love and the ability to love require one to be self-possessed and have self-control. Abiding love is not found in being controlled by and a slave to one's hormones and emotions. Here, we must agree that love is more than a chemical reaction and emotional high, and that you want to be both loved and to have some person(s) worthy of your love.

One has to give oneself away in order to love, and one cannot give that which one does not possess. Love is about both the self and the "other," and with mature love, it is in giving that one receives. As an example, God loves the souls in hell. The problem is that they chose not to love Him; they are incapable of a love outside of themselves. I do not suggest that those who lack love are incapable of passion, for they are fully capable of passions. But love is not *only* a passion. Love is also a decision, an act of the will. "Love is patient and kind; love does not envy or boast; it is not arrogant or rude. It does not insist on its own way; it is not irritable or resentful; it does not rejoice at wrongdoing, but *rejoices with the truth*" (1 Corinthians 13:4-6 ESV). Mature human love, which is a reflection of God's love, requires a *joy in the Truth*. The love that heals includes a deep personal concern that is open to, and perhaps even includes, a longing to give sacrificially for another, or to take another's pain, alienation, and sufferings on oneself. Love is the exact opposite of "it's all about me." Love is a virtue and calls for sacrifice. Children, teenagers, and adults know instinctively that they want to love and be loved! Of course, we can settle for sex, drugs, and rock and roll, or power, praise, and prestige; some may even be convinced by its apparent absence that love does not really exist, but it does. God is love.

You cannot love what you do not know said St. Thomas Aquinas. God is the source of love. The Cross of Christ is a powerful symbol of God's merciful love for sinners. He pours this love into the human heart through grace. But to deny Truth—objective, moral, knowable, eternal truth—is to deny love and believe a lie.

> **To deny Truth– objective, moral, knowable, eternal truth–is to deny love and believe a lie.**

5

An Internal Polarization

So what is God's plan for sex? I must begin with a clear confession that members of the Church, by word and deed, have failed to teach it well. In the course of teaching/ preaching the message of this book, I have had people remark to me, "Why haven't I been told this before?" What follows are a few of the reasons many Catholics have never really been told what the Church teaches, and why.

Several decades ago, some Catholic "experts" began a campaign to radically change and transform the teachings of the Catholic Church regarding sex and contraception. I am sure they had practical reasons, like the Protestants did, and believed the promised miracles of the Pill. These individuals wanted Catholicism to *get with the times* just as the Anglicans, Methodists, Baptists, Presbyterians, Evangelicals, Hindus, the Supreme Court, the United States Congress, etc., had done. A lot of Catholics were swayed by their inviting and progressive agenda presented with zeal, but it was a campaign of error, division, and half-truths. A few progressive Catholics even sought to show real "leadership" and get *ahead of the times* by pioneering what were then truly radical *new* ways in sexual teaching—embracing same-sex relationships and lowering the age of consent, but I am getting ahead of myself once again.

With the "progress" of the sexual revolution underway, those Catholics who desperately wanted the Church to be up to date and in on the new sexual times were in for a disappointment. In 1968, Pope Paul VI released a *restatement* of official Church teaching which explicitly *reiterated* that artificial contraception is a sin (misses the mark). Paul VI's statement is a letter titled *Humanae Vitae (Of Human Life)*. To say the least, *Humanae Vitae* was not well received by most members of the intellectual community and young Catholics, including some of those in seminaries. The "better" life, the promised fruits of contraception, the Protestant and near universal embrace of artificial birth control, women's liberation theology, ecology, and fascination with all things new worked against an obedient acceptance of this scriptural, ancient, and now counterintuitive teaching.

Misleading the Flock

Sadly, men and women (often priests, nuns, and teachers) called to understand, explain, and defend Church teaching instead got swept up in the sea of change. In order to facilitate "progress," the Church's constant understanding of both Scripture and natural law were attacked from within. Parts of Sacred Scripture were ignored or shaded and natural law was abandoned. Overwhelmed and with fading confidence, some Catholic pastors and teachers simply stood in a confused silence rather than effectively sharing the constant moral teaching of Catholicism. Other teachers and pastors proudly refuted Christian sexual morality in word and deed. Tragically, a few bishops "officially" rejected the Tradition of the Church and the Pope's authority. While not the only catalyst, these actions helped to usher in an age of great dissent, division, decline, disobedience, priest shortages, empty convents, confusion, silence, sexual immorality, and scandal, *the fruit of which is upon us.*

It is impossible for the level of incompetence demonstrated in some areas of Church leadership to have been accidental, and it wasn't. To deny any one teaching of the Church, such as Her teaching on contraception/sexual morality, requires a denial of so many more teachings. *All truth fits together.* The scale and the reach of this internal division should not be underestimated. In some places, speculative psychology was championed over fundamental theology, syndromes over sin. Tradition had to be discarded and authority rejected. Scripture and prayer had to be retranslated (and in some cases

> # It is impossible for the level of incompetence demonstrated in some areas of Church leadership to have been accidental, and it wasn't.

mistranslated). Teachings on morality and Church authority were stripped of substance. Sexual sin was ignored and the existence of hell denied. Without actually saying it or even admitting it to themselves, in the minds of many of Her clergy, nuns, and teachers the following position was lived: The Church is not only behind the times, but also wrong.

In the plan of a certain stripe of "progressive" Catholics, the Church became the enemy of progress and human fulfillment, and thus an object of scorn and bitter internal attack. Furthermore, the Church became an incubator for passive-aggressive self-loathing. Why would one dedicate his or her life to an institution with **clearly stated, deeply rooted, fundamental principles** which one utterly rejects? Imagine a pacifist enlisting in the Marine Corps infantry because he likes socialized medicine, military parades, and men in uniform. All too obviously, in certain cases this did not make for the best screening of or educating priests and perpetuating the faith.

> So many adult Catholics do not know the faith because what they were instructed in was presented as unnecessary, incomprehensible, and contradictory.

An embrace of the Church's clearly stated, deeply rooted, fundamental principles became labeled "rigidity" in places and was a reason to be rejected from the seminary or denied tenure at a university. Sexual confusion and moral ambivalence were seen as "openness." It has been a disaster and we are living it still. The sex-abuse crisis which erupted in 2002 is the one bad fruit that the media and general public will acknowledge and often use to further undermine respect for the Church and Her teachings.

St. John Chrysostom—who lived during the fourth and fifth centuries—soberly stated that the road to hell is paved with the skulls of erring priests and illuminated with the skulls of erring bishops. I soberly state that in recent decades the skulls of perverse priests may have joined them. *Never have so few done so much to destroy the faith of so many.* And so, this state of affairs has done its damage. The fullness of the faith simply has not been taught in places, and its substitute was a jumbled patchwork of watered-down "gospel" and secular philosophy. So many adult Catholics do not know the faith because what they were instructed in was presented as unnecessary, incomprehensible, and contradictory. Consequently, very many people have left the faith. Most have drifted away, some have been driven away, and some have quite rightly seen that their parish or priest or school was teaching neither the fundamentals nor the fullness of Christianity and sought it elsewhere. Of course there have been a few Catholics who have been faithfully given the full scope of the Church's teaching and still left Her flock; however, I believe they are the minority.

From the day Judas became the treasurer of the Twelve Apostles, the Church has had to deal with attacks from within and without. In this latest crisis of internal attacks a corner is being turned. Most recently-ordained priests have no interest in conforming the Church to the world's morality concerning sex. Also, some priests and teachers who previously embraced or tolerated contraception have experienced a change of heart.

There is no place for spiritual pacifists. Recently, a pastor I know told me he was trained in the early 1970s in the seminary to undermine the moral teaching of the Church on sex, and he was told (lied to, or at best misinformed) that in due time the official teachings would change. He believed the error he was taught and that in due time the Church would change. Today, his experiences with the destruction of the family and disorder in the Church's wider culture have helped him on his journey of conversion to the authentic, clear, and timeless moral teachings of the Church. He is now a strong advocate of God's mercy and a prophet of the dire, gradual consequences of sexual sin. Finally he is a gentle advocate of the need to teach the whole truth.

This is a spiritual battle. Each person must individually choose a side and fight accordingly. There is no place for spiritual pacifists. The enemies of Christ and His Church are not "flesh and blood" but falsehood and lies, evil spirits, principalities, and powers (see Ephesians 6:12). Still, teaching errors and/or half-truths is a root problem extending to the trunk and branches, and again, the resulting confusion and disobedience have borne bad fruit in every area of the Church: from the behavior of Catholics—single, married, priests, and religious—to broken lives and scandalized, scattered faithful.

The Latin proverb, *corruptio optimi pessima*, states that the corruption of the best is the worst. If one believes that Jesus founded a Church to "Go, therefore, and make disciples of all nations, baptizing them in the name of the Father, and of the Son, and of the Holy Spirit, teaching them to observe all that I have commanded you" (Matthew 28:19-20), then the corruption of that teaching is the worst of all corruptions, and must be recognized as a place of intense attack in the spiritual war of this life. Furthermore, if the family is "the best" environment to learn love, discipline, and self-control then the undermining of the family is the worst of all corruptions in the human drama. No ignorance, no neglect, no lukewarmness in "the best" will go unexploited by the Evil which is prowling around the world seeking the ruin of souls.

Corruptio optimi pessima.

6

What is True?

What does the Church _really_ teach about sex and marriage?

Your body is holy. Sexual relations between a husband and wife are a precious, holy, and blessed gift from God. The essence of love is to give. Your life, your body, and your spirit are gifts to you and are to be given, in turn, back to God, your spouse, your children, and the world. Self-control and discipline are both possible and necessary. God's intention is for men and women to reserve sex for marriage. The wedding night is to be an unveiling, a revelation of new intimacy and communion never before experienced. Sex **Your body is holy.** after the exchange of vows is actually the consummation (completion) of the wedding vows. In a very real sense, the wedding ceremony is not over until the verbal vows are lived in the exchange of persons, that is, bodily union;

Sex after the exchange of vows is actually the consummation of the wedding vows.

in a word, sex. Sex "seals the deal," so to speak. This time of powerful intimacy—this communion of persons—is to be a strong, holy bond in itself. Sex after the vows is a *reinforcement and renewal* of the promises and bond of the marriage ceremony.

The gift of self and sex in married life is to be a physical expression of married love: free, full, fruitful, and faithful. In the context of sex this means the following:

- Free—Not taken, not given under compulsion, not in lust, not for profit, not in trade, not in manipulation, but freely given by husband and wife.
- Full—Physical, emotional, and spiritual, without chemical or physical barriers or emotional reservations.
- Fruitful—Open to life, life-giving. Every sexual act is to be open to life and a renewal of the wedding consummation. Conception need not be sought and may even be impossible due a woman's cycle, illness, or age, but the door to fruitfulness is not to be "artificially" closed.
- Faithful—Sex is for marriage. Because sex is sacred, powerful, and life-giving, the sexual embrace is always reserved for one man and one woman publicly committed to one another in a permanent and stable relationship, ordered toward providing for and educating their offspring. In Christianity this relationship is "marriage."

Christian Marriage is a vocation—a calling from God—and, for those called, it is an aid to Christian perfection. Jesus raised marriage between the baptized to the dignity of a *sacrament*. Our source of grace is Jesus Christ, who gave us the sacraments as means of blessing, strengthening, and enriching us with the grace He merited on the cross. Marriage is not an end in and of itself but a means to an end (holiness). Sex is not an end in and of itself but a means of mutual self-giving between a husband and wife. Husband and wife are to be an image of Jesus' self-giving love for His Church and an example to the world. Sex is to be a joy, a pleasure, and a source of new life in the hearts of husband and wife and, perhaps, in pregnancy.

In marriage, God invites man and woman to participate in the act of the creation of a human life and an immortal soul. Sex is a religious act because of its connection to God and the exchange of persons and, therefore, has the potential of being profaned, that is, treated as "common" or without reverence. The act of treating something holy as if it were common or with contempt is to profane it. You and your body are to be holy, special. Sex is to be holy and special. Profaning sex is a serious sin.

Even the Best Marriages are Challenging

Marriage is a very difficult vocation, even with the help of God's grace and joyful, holy sex. The difficulty of marriage is rooted in fallen nature (remember our inclinations to throw others under the bus and fall off the wagon). Emotional and/or sexual fidelity *will be tested and tried* in the overwhelming majority of marriages. The marriage *vows* are solemn promises witnessed and sealed by God to love and honor in "good times and bad, sickness and health," and the grace of the sacrament will be called upon over and over. Laws, principles, and vows are most important in times of temptation, when body and soul rise in mutiny against the Way, when veins run with fire and the heart beats with uncountable throbs. Then, at that hour, preconceived opinions and foregone determinations are all one has, and there you must plant your foot, so said Jane Eyre.

Sex outside of marriage is a destructive sin. Marriage is all the more difficult when the husband and wife have been unfaithful to each other, *even if the infidelity took place before they were married or even before they met*. Minds are filled with memories, misconceptions, heartbreak, and broken promises made and received. I ask teenagers and young adults, "Do you want a happy marriage, a loving and faithful wife or husband, and a peace-filled home?" Of course they answer, "Yes." The obvious instruction is, "Go and sin no more." This instruction

---

Marriage is not an end in and of itself but a means to an end (holiness). Sex is not an end in and of itself but a means of mutual self-giving between a husband and wife.

> # Marriage is all the more difficult when the husband and wife have been unfaithful to each other, even if the infidelity took place before they were married.

is simple and yet, particularly in our day and time, far from easy. Remember, too, that Jesus came to heal sinners and make all things new. "Bad choices" and the lingering scars of sexual sin can be healed, but it requires grace, time, prayer, and trust. Here, the old saying applies, "An ounce of prevention is worth a pound of cure."

Some say that Christian teaching is centered on "no." However, behind any "no" that is a part of the Christian message there are many "yeses." Yes to fidelity, yes to love, yes to honor, yes to life, yes to holiness, yes to self-control, yes to permanence, yes to purpose, yes to health, yes to happiness, and yes to following Jesus.

What the Church Does Not Teach

The Church does *not* teach that a couple *must* have children or every child possible. The Church teaches that married couples should be open to children. Potential parents are called, that is, required, to prayerfully consider the principle of responsible parenthood. When serious physical, medical, financial, or psychological reasons are present, couples are permitted to take advantage of natural means/cycles to limit their family size. This process is called "Natural Family Planning." It's free or virtually free, effective, and morally acceptable. Natural Family Planning requires a little training, an accurate thermometer, a simple chart, and observations. Natural Family Planning embraces the science of fertility and a life of grace.

True, Natural Family Planning also calls for these intangibles: trust in God, trust in one's beloved, prayer, communication, understanding, patience, sacrifice, a proper understanding of sex, obedience and, at times, "the Cross." ("The Cross" is the pain of doing the right thing in the face of tremendous temptation or persecution.) Giving and receiving these gifts with heart and soul are truly what make a marriage holy, happy, and lasting.

Natural Family Planning encourages the man and the woman to be mutually responsible for their combined fertility. It will not always be easy, but it is possible. Again, sex is intended to be holy, and Natural Family Planning respects and embraces this truth. Natural Family Planning is much easier when the couple learned to love and communicate without depending on sex during courtship.

One argument against using Natural Family Planning is that it is the equivalent of sterilization and contraception. But if that's the case, then why not use Natural Family Planning? With this question, it becomes clear that these methods are not equal. Rather, the intended consequences—the ends—are very similar. But we must remember that, for the Christian, sex is not the ultimate goal. Holiness is, perfection is, and beatitude is. To say Natural Family Planning and contraception are the same is to say that anorexia and fasting are the same, or liposuction and exercise are the same, or that robbing the wealthy to give to the poor is the same as generosity. It is a lie to say they are equivalent.

Natural Family Planning does work, and not only does it work, it does not disturb the delicate hormonal processes that occur in a woman's body or cause problems for children conceived while the mother has these extra chemicals in her body. Additionally, studies suggest that a woman on the Pill (or other hormonal contraceptives) may become less appealing to her partner because of the hormones she emanates.

Furthermore, there is evidence that the birth control hormones that pass through a woman and into our waterways harm wildlife. Natural Family Planning respects God's plan for the true holiness of sex and for God's broader creation.

On the other hand, contraception moves heterosexual sex in the direction of homosexual sex and opens people to the idea of unnaturally sterile sex. Once again, I am getting ahead of myself.

> # Natural Family Planning calls for trust in God, trust in one's beloved, prayer, communication, patience, a proper understanding of sex, and "the Cross."

Lies and Consequences

When God's plan and the holiness of sex are discarded the unintended consequences can be devastating. Among Catholics who practice Natural Family Planning, with both the husband and wife on board, the divorce rate is tiny. For the remainder of couples in the United States, the rate soars to near 50% (Centers for Disease Control and Prevention, "National Marriage and Divorce Rate Trends"), not to mention couples who "shack up" and then break up. Today, so many people experience divorce and/or abandonment—a disaster for both them and society. Don't believe anything to the contrary. Keep in mind that, since human beings are composite beings of body and soul, "junk sex" has both spiritual and bodily consequences.

> # Contraception moves heterosexual sex in the direction of homosexual sex.

Somewhat Innocent Bystander

I believe that many people who have used contraception in marriage are in some ways subjectively innocent. In other words, they do not or did not really have sufficient knowledge to understand that contraception is a sin that damages their spiritual health and the lives of their family members and society. *Yet even when there is a degree of innocence because of ignorance, sin still destroys.* Sin is like a poison. Sin—even in ignorance—creates a kind of gravitational pull away from truth, grace, and the Church. Sin—even in ignorance—still weakens the will and sows destructive seeds in lives, families, and communities. It kills. "The wages of sin is death" (Romans 6:23). But thanks be to Jesus Christ who comes to free us from sin. For this reason it is important to know and share the fullness of the faith. God wants us to be saved and come to knowledge of the truth. Fortunately, there are more educational resources available than ever before—in addition to graces from prayer, spiritual and other types of counseling, and the sacraments—to assist us in working toward the beatitude that we all seek and which God desires for us.

"I know that most men, including those at ease with problems of the greatest complexity, can seldom accept even the simplest and most obvious truth if it be such as would oblige them to admit the falsity of conclusions which they delighted in explaining to colleagues, which they have proudly taught to others, and which they have woven, thread by thread, into the fabric of their lives."

- Leo Tolstoy

A Question of Truth

Am I saying the key to happiness is having alot of children? No, not necessarily so. Some of the keys to happiness are gratitude, self-control, generosity, and a purpose in life.

- Gratitude—Perpetually conscious that life is a precious gift, difficult as it may be at times, and full of desire to fulfill one's destiny in God's Kingdom—both on earth and in eternity.
- Self-control—Not being under the dominion of bodily appetites or the desire for accolades and approval;

being beyond the manipulation of advertisers and popular opinion.

- Generosity—Giving of time, talent, and treasure; life and limb, even to the point of sacrifice in pursuit of the good of others toward a noble and enduring purpose.

In the realm of sex and marriage, these qualities bring purity outside of marriage and an openness to life within marriage.

There is then the question of truth. A turn away from individualism, materialism, and consumerism must be directed toward something else. The turn from the false ideal of "more stuff for me equals happiness," if it is a healthy step toward happiness, can't be a turn to "nothingness" or "pointlessness" (although nihilism, a rejection of all moral principles and an embrace of the belief that life is meaningless, is a common pitfall for those in a life of sexual sin).

What is noble? Is a large family noble? What is worth sacrifice...are children? Could part of one's purpose be to build up the Kingdom of God, establishing and providing for a family? If one answers yes, then perhaps being open to more than one or two or three children is both a path to happiness and the result of the pursuit of happiness.

Having lots of children without gratitude, self-control, and generosity could make for misery for the parents and children. Hopefully, that misery would become a catalyst to seek the truth, to seek the way, and to find the virtues that lead to God, to beatitude.

St. Paul on What is True

St. Paul gives a summary of what the Catholic Church

still teaches today in his letter to the Corinthians. This letter was written about 2,000 years ago to the men and women of Corinth in Greece. Corinth was a city where sex was not seen as holy in the Christian sense; rather, sex was simply for pleasure or at times part of pagan worship or self-worship. Furthermore, excess in food, alcohol, and sex were corrupting the Christian community. Paul writes this warning and challenge to them and it is perfectly suited to our situation today.

> Do you not know that the unjust will not inherit the kingdom of God? Do not be deceived; neither fornicators nor idolaters nor adulterers nor boy prostitutes nor sodomites [people having homosexual sex] nor thieves nor the greedy nor drunkards nor slanderers nor robbers will inherit the kingdom of God. That is what some of you used to be; but now you have had yourselves washed [baptized], you were sanctified, you were justified in the name of the Lord Jesus Christ and in the Spirit of our God.

> "Everything is lawful for me," but not everything is beneficial. "Everything is lawful for me," but I will not let myself be dominated by anything. "Food for the stomach and the stomach for food," but God will do away with both the one and the other. The body, however, is not for immorality, but for the Lord, and the Lord is for the body; God raised the Lord and will also raise us by his power. Do you not know that your bodies are members of Christ? Shall I then take Christ's members and make them the members of a prostitute? Of course not! [Or] do you not know that anyone who joins himself to a prostitute becomes one body with her? For "the two," it says, "will become one flesh." But whoever is joined to the Lord becomes one spirit with him. Avoid immorality. Every other sin a person commits is outside the body, but the immoral person sins against his own body.

Do you not know that your body is a temple of the Holy Spirit within you, whom you have from God, and that you are not your own? For you have been purchased at a price. Therefore, glorify God in your body (1 Corinthians 6:9-20).

Sin—even in ignorance—still weakens the will and sows destructive seeds in lives, families, and communities. It kills.

7

Promises and Prophecy

Do you recall the promises of the Pill? Happiness, pleasure, license, freedom from responsibility, fewer divorces, better marriages, fewer—if any—abortions, no unwanted children, fewer single mothers, happier women, happier society, and better sex, especially for women.

Life is difficult. Life includes suffering. There is no escaping these facts.

Running from the suffering of this life is not the path to happiness. In fact, running from the legitimate difficulties, disciplines, sorrows, and sufferings of life often leads to vice, addiction, a personal sense of abandonment, and confusion about one's purpose and destiny. These things are life's greatest darkness and lead to death, both spiritual and physical.

Self-control is a difficult, exacting, and life-long project. Respecting the holiness of sex is a challenge; therefore, teaching the holiness and purpose of both sex and the human body convincingly has always been a challenge. But

> # Running from the legitimate difficulties, disciplines, sorrows, and sufferings of life often leads to vice, addiction, a personal sense of abandonment.

today, teaching against contraception and adultery is counter-cultural and "rebellious" in certain quarters, but it must be proclaimed from the watchtower regardless. Taught and lived, this doctrine makes the Church like a light on a hill in a world going dark. When the Catholic Church and Her teachings on sex and the body are clearly seen, She becomes both a target of persecution and a destination for those seeking true freedom. "Whoever is not with me is against me, and whoever does not gather with me scatters," said Jesus (Luke 11:23).

Modern Prophecy

"Seeing" the future in light of God's truth and predicting what is going to happen is a kind of prophecy. Pope Paul VI predicted that several things would happen as the world and individuals embraced contraception. Perhaps the easiest prediction to see as having been fulfilled is his assertion that as contraception becomes more common there will be a general lowering of morality, especially among the young.

Contraceptive use among children and adults has launched a lifestyle of fornication. Fornication, which is sex with

46

someone you are not married to, is a form of adultery (serious sin). Here it is helpful to remember these things:

- A sin is to miss, be wrong, go in the wrong direction, an offense against love, truth, and right reason.
- The goal of human nature is to love and be loved.

Kids have always been curious about sex and throughout history some have experimented, but now they have been given a license to act on their impulses. Contraceptive use has authorized sexual license, and instead of healing us and our kids of disordered impulses, it has lowered moral standards, sown confusion about the meaning of sex, and made our disordered impulses both more acute and more likely to be acted upon.

Human beings most often live up or down to what is expected of them. Blame it on the lowering of morality. Parenting today, for many, is to give kids condoms or put teenage daughters on the Pill, which is a kind of emotional death sentence. Parents and other adults see this as necessary because they are convinced that children who have been given a bad example, and whose parents have told them *nothing* about the holiness or purpose of sex, are *going* to act out. When did Americans go from assuming that the majority of kids, given love and taught virtue, could control their behavior; to assuming that we are all out of control and enslaved to lust?

With lowered morality,

> # Human beings most often live up or down to what is expected of them.

virtue (defined as a good habit of the mind or body that enables one to easily do the "right thing") is for too many a forgotten or never-learned concept. As a general rule, kids have always had lapses in reliability, from taking out the trash to finishing homework on time. Children need special attention and training to grow in virtue; this is one of a parent's chief responsibilities. But without training in virtue or an appreciation of the power and sacredness of sex, we have an epidemic of teenage sex, teen moms, teen abortions, abuse, dysfunction, divorce, depression, and disease.

Movies, video games, TV shows, and advertisements constantly trivialize and glamorize fornication and adultery, objectify the body, and encourage acting out. One need only compare today's television, movies, fashions, and magazines to those of 50 years ago. That which not long ago would have been clearly seen as provocative and seductive is the steady diet of most modern Americans. Is there any wonder so many kids and adults struggle to live the virtue of self-control?

Modesty, an attractive and simple elegance that shuns the superficial, is an especially forgotten virtue. Dressing modestly and beautifully draws attention and respectful admiration, but

> Dressing modestly and beautifully draws attention and respectful admiration, but publicly displaying one's flesh hoping for a "fix" of attention is the definition of superficial.

publicly displaying one's flesh hoping for a "fix" of attention is the definition of superficial. Predictably, superficiality is where so many modern relationships, even marriages, live and die. But the love you crave, especially as you mature, is intimate, blessed, patient, kind, rejoicing in the truth—*not* superficial.

A Telling Snapshot

In Peter Kreeft's book, *Making Choices: Practical Wisdom for Everyday Moral Decisions,* he tells of a 1958 survey that asked high school principals, "What are the main problems among your students?" The top answers were as follows: 1) not doing homework, 2) not respecting property (e.g., throwing books), 3) leaving lights on, doors and windows open, 4) throwing spitballs, 5) running in halls. The same survey given in 1988 yielded much different results: 1) abortion, 2) AIDS, 3) rape, 4) drugs, 5) fear of violence (guns, weapons at schools). Clearly the focus of the answers changed from "the problems your kids cause" to "the challenges they deal with and bring to school"; but even that aspect of the survey tells a tragic tale. Our children really have become victims of their parents' pursuit of pleasure.

I do not need to bore you with statistics. Simply look at your life, family, friends, classroom, child's classroom, and workplace. I call it "name soup." Who is the daddy of whom; how many half-siblings are living together with virtual strangers; who, if anyone, is providing for, protecting, and teaching the children to be virtuous? In the broken home there is almost always an acute absence of a man to teach his sons virtue.

Marriage has as its greatest goods the holiness of the spouses and the life and education of children, the opposite of "it's all about me." Parents, united in marriage, are principally responsible for the education of their children. The state may be available to help the parents, and the state may or may not seek to destroy the Christian virtue of children. The demands of "social justice" on behalf of children include self-giving, risk, sacrifice, love, and the example of virtue; these also are means of self-growth and satisfaction with one's life and purpose...happiness.

> In the broken home there is almost always an acute absence of a man to teach his sons virtue.

Wanting Children, Like Wanting Pets

In modern marriage, the mindset, "I want one boy and one girl to complete *my life*" is common, even if it is subconcious. Too many potential parents in the modern world believe marriage is all about the adults, and children are somehow ornaments on the adults' lives. "It's all about me." Family planning is like pet shopping: one dog and one cat. Natural Family Planning counters this mindset and often opens couples to the idea of the generosity of welcoming more children and building the Kingdom of God in and through their family while growing in trust of God.

Freedom or Slavery

There can be no freedom in the absence of virtue. Virginia Woolf said, "To enjoy freedom we have to control ourselves." What woman would want to marry a man who could not control his sexual desire even when she "has a headache"? What man would want to marry a woman with no self-control, even when he is off at work? "Only a virtuous people are capable of freedom. As nations become corrupt and vicious, they have more need of masters," said Benjamin Franklin.

We live in a world with many millions of emotionally enslaved, confused, neglected, and sexually active or abused kids/adults, and on top of these wounds, most have been given very little understanding of discipline in virtue or the purpose of sex and their bodies.

Adultery and divorce have given rise to whole generations living in broken homes who are desperate for stability, affection, and acceptance; a divorced, never married, or unfaithful dad and/or mom who is out scratching the itch of his or her libido (sex drive) does not make for happy, virtuous, or safe kids. Divorce and abandonment really are endangering and devastating to children and their happiness, even once they become adults. Remember that even adults are someone's child.

> # As sex is easier to get, the virtue of love is harder to find.

For many teens, sex is almost a given as part of their desperate groping for love and affection. In some cases, genital sex is viewed as being as insignificant (or even less significant) then holding hands once was. Some kids engage in sex with the hope that someone will care enough even to hold their hands.

As sex is easier to get, the virtue of love is harder to find. As true affection is traded for fleeting pleasure, sex is too often employed as the easy way—a fix—to soothe or drown out the confusion and disorder of a broken life, in much the same way as are drugs and alcohol.

Beauty and Magnetism

There is nothing more attractive and beautiful than the human body. Few things are more satisfying than an affectionate and welcomed touch from a familiar person. In addition to the simple physical beauty of the human body, there is a spiritual dimension and biological impulse contributing to the attraction between the sexes. On top of these good and powerful draws, children entering adolescence today are surrounded and invaded by an unholy stew of artificial hormones, chemicals, the graphic images of the Internet, movies, poor parental guidance, and encouragement in some quarters that teenagers acting out sexually is healthy, normal, and expected.

> There is nothing more attractive and beautiful than the human body.

What was once for most a time of curiosity, naiveté, and emotional, psychological, and sexual immaturity has given rise to more and more oral, anal, and/or vaginal sexual acting out with friends, strangers, and predators of either or both sexes—sometimes even animals.

There is a bond that comes with the sexual act, at least initially, which makes "the other" even more attractive. Instead of kids and young adults maturing through what may well have been fleeting sexual immaturity, confusion, or curiosity, more and more kids are being encouraged to embrace themselves as gay or bisexual, and therefore part of a special interest group with privileges and a certain uniqueness. In a world always looking for the next novelty, we have an increasing number of girls and boys, men and women whose sexual disorders include sexual addiction, homosexual confusion, homosexual acting out, and unhealthy (and ultimately unhappy) attachments based on the sexual bond.

Young couples, rather than thoughtfully and clearheadedly choosing a partner as was promised by the Pill, are sliding into weak marriages or "shacking up" based on sex and convenience. On a very basic level, the sexual embrace (easy intimacy and communication, pleasure, and mutual acceptance of sex) can make people feel as though they are in love when they don't even know each other, or themselves. This makes for an explosion of terrible parents and dysfunctional homes. These add up to less happiness no matter how much stuff one has.

More Stuff in the Home and Less Room in the Heart

It is true that the culture of contraception has often meant fewer children, more sexual partners, and more material possessions for many. On the other hand, more work today very often means more time away from home and less stable, more self-centered marriages. Add to this a vasectomy or tubal ligation (tied tubes), an attractive coworker, a business trip or lunch on the heels of a little tension at home, and the door for an affair is kicked wide, wide open. A husband once told me getting a vasectomy was like getting a new toy (and not just for home use). On another occasion, a woman stated bluntly that she had her tubes tied so she could cheat on her husband.

Most Americans today enjoy food, medicine, conveniences, and entertainment unimagined by all but the wealthiest around the world until just a century ago, but what do we hear? We hear a constant mantra of "these tough economic times." Material prosperity and emotional poverty coexist— the paradox of having more and less at the same time—while parents, step-parents, and step-grandparents work "just to make ends meet." They work to pay the daycare, child support, alimony, attorney, nursing home, and, of course, to buy the $200 shoes. Abraham Lincoln lived in a dirt-floored house much of his childhood, possessing only three books, but he had parents (and eventually a step-mother) who loved him. He was reared in material poverty but was rich in virtue.

Today, there are many homes where nobody is working and mom is living hand-to-mouth off of government hand-outs or "disability." The number of undereducated single mothers has skyrocketed in the age of contraception, abortion, and government programs operating to "assist" them. The government can't fix these problems by providing free birth control. True virtue and purpose do not come from a pill.

There are still homes where children are taught about the holiness of sex and the gifts of truth, beauty, and goodness. There are loving parents who teach the consequences of sin and discipline their children appropriately. These are mostly happy homes. These are the families that kids naturally gravitate towards. Of course, some kids reared in the best environment may still stray, and others with all the odds against them may remain models of virtue and self-control; nevertheless, it should be becoming clear why our living rooms and classrooms are in the state they are in.

> # True virtue and purpose do not come from a pill.

8

Women

An amazingly beautiful young divorcée whom I know well told me she showed up at a family holiday meal all alone—no man. Her uncle asked her if she was alone and then declared her "wasted meat." She has never forgotten that snapshot of his impression of her value. Spoken or unspoken, this is the way too many men appraise the value of too many girls and women, and highlights the truth of another of Pope Paul VI's prophecies. He said that widespread contraception would bring about "a general disregard for the physical and psychological well-being of females by males." Contraception may not have started this, but it certainly has made it worse! One might simply ask whether there is more or less pornography today than in the 1960s, more or fewer strip joints, more or less sexual abuse, more or less sex trafficking, more or less prostitution. The statistics concerning the number of women who have suffered some type of sexual abuse are staggering. Varying data indicate that from one in ten to *one in three* women will experience some form of sexual abuse during their youth. I am inclined to believe it is very likely one in three. Pornography—live, in print, on video, and particularly via the Internet—is everywhere, and the *objectification* of human persons, especially women, is celebrated in a culture of pornography. People are supposed to be loved and not used as objects. The devastating effects of sexual objectification with its reduction of one's value to "used" or "wasted" meat are incalculable—even when the one being "used" is being paid or "chooses" to be used.

I have been told that many women in the sex industry turn to other women for emotional and sexual intimacy because their whole paradigm of male sex is one of objectification, use, and abuse. This reality applies not just to "professionals" but also to little girls who began to be seduced from their first week of puberty or before. Sadly, many women are permanently "turned off" or bizarrely promiscuous because they have been lied to, groped, used, abused, neglected, and/or had one or more abortions.

Many men (and some women) prefer cyber-sex to sex with their spouses. Men have "imprinted" on sexual images based on fantasy and not the face, smile, and body of their wives. Wives report that it seems at times that the husband is simply masturbating inside of them while a million miles away emotionally.

No sane person needs to be convinced she wants to be happy.

Are mothers, daughters, wives, and sisters happier after the contraception-fueled sexual revolution? Maureen Dowd, a malformed Catholic who insults the faith each time she claims it, addresses something like this question in an article she wrote for the *New York Times* titled, "Blue is the New Black" (September 19, 2009). In Ms. Dowd's article she makes the following points, often quoting researchers and experts:

- In the early '70s, young women, leaving their mothers' limited lives behind, felt exhilarated and bold.
- Amazingly, women *are not just like men*; they have more feelings.
- Before the '70s, there was a gender gap in America in which women felt greater well being. Now, there's a gender gap in which men feel better about their lives.
- It doesn't matter what their marital status is, how much money they make, whether or not they have children, their ethnic background, or the country they live in. Women around the world are in a funk.
- Choice is inherently stressful.
- Women are being driven to distraction.
- Women have lives that become increasingly empty.
- America is more youth obsessed and looks [sex] obsessed than ever.
- On the bright side of the dark trend she contends, *happiness is beside the point.*
- We're "happy" to have our newfound abundance of choices, even if those choices end up making us unhappier.

I remind you that *no sane person needs to be convinced she wants to be happy* and that a sane person likewise desires happiness for her children. *Happiness is not beside the point.* The choice to be unhappy, I think, is one key to the mystery of how a good God could have people go to hell; they really do freely go to their "own place" holding fast to their choices and errors, in some respects choosing to be slaves to their choices. As they go, God is wooing them all the while: "Come to me, all you that are weary and are carrying heavy burdens, and I will give you rest. Take my yoke upon you, and learn from me; for I am gentle and humble in heart, and you will find rest for your souls" (Matthew 11:28-29).

My life's observations confirm an idea I heard from Bishop Fulton Sheen. He said that the two major causes of mental unhappiness are: 1) unrequited guilt and 2) want of a purpose in life. Freedom is not in the number of choices one has; rather, freedom is in being able to choose the best purpose and the ability to navigate the Way without falling victim to the Siren song of the lesser choices.

One more point worth noting is that Ms. Dowd offers only a single veiled solution. She suggests that actually having children makes women even unhappier. I don't think Ms. Dowd gets it. Sex and "choice" do not a purpose make; and if one's heart is not dead, some choices bring guilt—even if that guilt remains mostly subconscious.

"I had sex last night and now I choose to kill my unborn child (or let the chemicals I put in my system flush him/her out) and pay for my Prozac on my own" is neither freedom nor happiness.

A young woman was quoted in Erin Ann McBride's article, "Where Have All the Real Men Gone?" (*Meridian* Magazine, October 9, 2012): "I know I am able to take care of myself. I have confidence in that. But it sure doesn't take away the desire to have someone to take care of me—a protector, someone who makes me feel safe physically and emotionally." I know it sounds old fashioned: An emotionally healthy woman wants one man to cherish, protect, and respect her. I do not believe that it is written into the female code, even under a fallen nature, to want a series of partners. She wants only one. A woman wants a man who is fun and funny, but when the laughs fade to real life, she wants a man who "*will be there for me.*" She can be convinced otherwise, and, unfortunately, far too many young women and not-so-young women **have** been persuaded differently. Yes, it is a great risk for a woman to even allow herself to desire a man possessing heroic virtue who will cherish and protect her in a world of frogs, but the solution is *not* to become just like a man.

> Freedom is not the number of choices one has; rather, freedom is in being able to choose the best purpose and the ability to navigate the Way without falling victim to the Siren song of the lesser choices.

9

Men

Personally, I think that some women are somewhat less than happy because of the men they have to choose from or have chosen, and because of what so many of their fathers, sons, and brothers have become in the oversexed, contraception-fueled world of today and the recent past. Too many sons of the first and second generation of "liberated women" are living a protracted adolescence, having been insulated from sharing and responsibility in their 1.5 child household or broken home. They were not properly disciplined, mothered, or fathered; they are now narcissistic, disrespectful, un-churched, ungrateful, and addicted to pornography, sterile sex, masturbation, video games, and sports...in a word, lost. Not exactly a portrait of a knight in shining armor, Prince Charming, or even a decent male human being.

At his best, every man wants to be a hero. He wants to provide and protect. He wants a woman to protect, one worthy of the laying down of his life. In his book, *Wild at Heart*, John Eldredge says that a man craves "an adventure to live," "a beauty to rescue," "a battle to fight." It is obvious that he can settle for beer, video games, porn, and self-gratification, but it is beneath what even pagan virtues call him to. The ideals of every civilization

> **Too many sons of the first and second generation of "liberated women" are living a protracted adolescence.**

from ancient Rome and the Greeks to the Chinese, Native Americans, and all points between called men to be self-controlled providers and protectors, in a word, heroes.

Men throughout history have had rites of passage as they progress from being a child, one who is provided for and protected, to a man, one who is providing and protecting. In some places, this was demonstrated by the courageous men who climbed the walls of the city to face the foes outside. The enemies were outside seeking to conquer the town, kill or enslave the men, and exploit the women and children. The women, children, and infirm were inside—protected by and supporting the social and physical structures of the community. Today, we face far fewer threats from the neighboring town or state attempting to invade with

64

intentions of conquering our walled city; rather, the battle men are called to fight today is to protect themselves, their wives, and their children from lies and sexual exploitation. Sadly, we live in a world where so many adult men are nothing more than adolescents—no longer up on the wall protecting their families and training the boys and young men; instead, they are seated in front of their computers or televisions with their genitals in their hands, welcoming—or even becoming—the very enemy which seeks to destroy the women and children in their homes and communities.

Contraception did not cause these problems in the world, it made them worse. The promises of the Pill were and are slick and empty, in a word, lies. Lies that enslave.

10
The Uninvited Guest: No Room in the Inn

With the contraceptive mindset, the unintentionally-conceived child constitutes an uninvited guest; literally, an unwelcome intruder. The mother's or father's attitude may be fear, anger, or selfishness. The thought—whether conscious or unconscious—is, at times, "This child will steal my freedom; I will be linked to this man/woman I do not want to be linked to; the pregnancy will take away my security, my new bass boat, my new kitchen, and my perky breasts. Carrying this child will tell on me, tell of my behavior or my experience, and I am afraid." Often these are the reasons why preborn babies are killed.

Until 1973 abortion was a crime and illegal in the USA. Before 1973 abortions were performed, but not a huge number. Since 1973 about 25% of the babies conceived in the United States have been killed. From 1973-2013 there were approximately 50,000,000 abortions *in the USA alone*. Try to wrap your mind around that number. Did you know that the 1992 *Planned Parenthood v. Casey* Supreme

> # Remember what an abortion is: the killing of an innocent being who happens to be wholly dependent on his or her mother.

Court ruling linked the lifestyle and choices available through contraception to a requirement for the availability of abortion? In other words, couples have chosen to have sex only because they can do so without concern about pregnancy. But we all know contraception fails at times; therefore, the Supreme Court mandated that abortion must be an option for the couple who uses contraception. This is the logic of the human law. Remember what an abortion is: the killing of an innocent human being who happens to be *wholly dependent* on his or her mother, an *unspeakable crime* (Vatican II).

Selling women abortion masquerading as "contraception" is a deceptive practice (a lie). Women need to know that today contraception is often abortion, not only because the third generation pills (hormones) currently prescribed do not necessarily just prevent sperm from fertilizing the egg; at times they prevent the tiny baby, with her own unique genome, from implanting in the uterus. As for IUDs, they definitively cause spontaneous abortions of fertilized eggs, and women who use them as contraceptives are actually being equipped with a do-it-yourself abortionist's tool. By the way, abortions caused by the pill and IUDs are not included in the figure of 50,000,000 quoted above.

Either one behaves as she believes or believes as she behaves. The Gospel of Luke tells us that Jesus was praised by John the Baptist within days of His conception in Mary's womb. As if to emphasize the point, this happened while John, too, was still in the womb of his mother, Elizabeth (Luke 1:39-45).

Contrast John's reaction to the arrival of Jesus to that of King Herod, who, in order to save himself future trouble, had many children in and around Bethlehem killed (Matthew 2:1-18). Herod acted as he did because of his belief that these babies posed a threat to his comfort, position, and power. Remember, Jesus said that His coming would cause division (Luke 12:51); our choices constitute our acceptance or our rejection of His Kingdom of love. Jesus challenged us to see that all we do (or fail to do) for the least of His brothers, we do to Him.

I have experienced as a confessor and counselor women's heartbreak at their actions committed in ignorance, fear, and desperation. I have seen them carrying their signs: "I regret my abortion" and "Abortion: One dead, one wounded." Remember that Jesus came to forgive sinners and that any sin can be forgiven, provided there is repentance. The devil, on the other hand, tries to persuade those involved in abortion

> # Selling women abortion masquerading as "contraception" is a deceptive practice.

to believe that there is no sin to forgive. Conversely, those burdened with guilt are tempted to disbelieve that God's tender love is ever present and that God's mercy infinitely surpasses the sin of abortion. To deny or bury the pain of killing your child is one type of the unacknowledged guilt I alluded to earlier, and another reason why women may be less content on average than they were in 1970.

> # "Abortion: One dead, one wounded."

Not Children to Love, But Choices to Make

When pregnancy is reduced to "choice," the child herself is soon reduced to a choice and humans start choosing options, seeking efficiency, and eliminating "defects." We now have a new word in the English language: gendercide. Gendercide is genocide but for one gender only.

Imagine waking up tomorrow to not a single female in the USA—not a single one, all dead. Mara Hvistendahl reports in her book, *Unnatural Selection*, that there have been so many sex-selection abortions in the past three decades that 160 million girls who should have been born are missing from the area in and around India and China. (There are about 320 million people in the United States and about half—160,000,000—are female.) She is still pro-abortion but apparently wants more baby boys killed. I don't think she gets it. I do not think "choice" has been good for our collective sanity or sanctity. I know that the absence of the gift and giftedness of those 160 million women to their families and cultures is going to have devastating and long-term effects. Furthermore, what are those 160 million men who lack marriage partners going to do with themselves? Hvistendahl predicts that those women who made it out of the womb will face increased threats from sex-trafficking, "bride-buying" (a euphemism for slavery-prostitution), and violence. Simply put, a shortage of women will mean more rape, bloodshed, and violence for women.

Gaia, the Earth Goddess

But for some people, there is yet another BIG problem being solved by sterile sex that I have only alluded to thus far. It is becoming such a widespread philosophy you might even have considered your personal benefits from its acceptance. Chicken Little was not the first to yell, "The sky is falling," and there have been doomsday predictions about many things, including overpopulation and scarcity, for a long, long, long time. But with the shrinking world, technological advances, travel, and improved health care, a kind of global overpopulation mentality has fallen from the sky and taken root. There was a movie in the '70s called *Soylent Green* in which humanity was forced to resort to cannibalism (imposed secretly by the government) because of scarcity. And perhaps you are thinking, as I once might have, that those 160 million female babies torn from their mothers' wombs would not be good for "the environment" if they had been born. Maybe you have taken it a step further and embraced the idea that "for the earth, for *me* and *my* offspring, *they* are better off dead." Beware of the Big Lie.

A famous and influential elected leader once said that people are more likely to believe a big lie than a little one, and if the lie is big enough, simple enough, and repeated often enough people will believe it. If the problem to be solved is scarcity of resources, the Big Lie is that there is not enough for everyone; thus human life is like a cancer on earth.

Global scarcity is part of the Big Lie.

The photographs and biographies of starving children or children in otherwise difficult situations are heartbreaking, but their circumstances are not simply the product of global or even local scarcity; rather, war, tribal feuds, government corruption, disasters, and man's inhumanity to man all contribute. Of course, all are called to good stewardship of the earth and must seek a living wage for even the poorest, but genocide/gendercide is never a solution.

Again, stewardship of natural resources is a serious issue, but global scarcity is part of the Big Lie. Concerns about nature, important though they may be, ought not lead to the conclusion on the part of a single believing Christian that, "For the good of the earth we can only responsibly have one or two children." Anyone willing to look critically at the data about scarcity and overpopulation will see that the real question is not "When we are going to run out?" The real questions are: What is the purpose of the earth and its resources? How will we be good stewards of the earth? What is the proper way to plan family size?

Recall God's exhortation to be fruitful and multiply and

fill the earth (Genesis 1:28 and 9:1). Scripture is a living word and applies to every age. Reflecting on God's generosity and faithfulness fills us with trust and hope as we answer God's call to use our gifts and talents in responding creatively and generously to the challenges of our day. Furthermore, if you have eyes to see, you should already recognize that earth worshippers and those consumed by the population-control gods will begin to sterilize themselves into annihilation. The problem is, they want everyone to worship their *gods*...but I am getting ahead of myself once again.

Have You Found Your Purpose and Higher Power?

Sooner or later, to the heart of every man and woman who truly seeks enlightenment, comes a rejection of Consumerism, Materialism, and Individualism as spiritual junk food that does not fulfill the supernatural longings of the human heart. Sadly, many who claim the name "Christian" never reach this state of insight.

I do not think it a weakness to admit I need a cause bigger than myself. In fact, every one of us needs something bigger than ourself, outside of ourself. This is part of our nature. For many, the god of the day is the earth—known in ancient times as Terra, in "New Age" terminology as Gaia. The worship of this god allows sexual immorality, impurity, sensuality, drunkenness, adultery, and divorce. Furthermore, this god often encourages sterility and promotes abortion. Of course this god also loves recycling and things like "Meatless Monday," a movement to abstain from meat one day a week to protect or in honor of the earth. Environmentalism is not bad, it is good—until it becomes the measure of all truth and thus the worship of a false god. Satan always imitates God and tries to make his deceptions seem like the Christian principles of sacrifice, love, stewardship, wisdom, beauty, etc.

Contraception, sterility, abortion, and homosexual acting out are about sex, but more than sex, they are about the purpose of life, the meaning of our bodies, truth, human relationships, creation, and the relationship between material (body) and spiritual (soul).

11

Natural Law

The truth can be known. It is that simple. We will be judged on our embrace and love of the Truth. Just as you are responsible for seeking happiness (beatitude), you are responsible for knowing and living the truth. The only good reason to believe in something is that it *is true*. It may be inconvenient to believe that a preborn child is an innocent human being with the same right to life as an adult, but it does not change the truth. Some people believe that somehow it is permissible to buy or sell and otherwise mistreat people as property, but that does not make it true. To reject the truth is a kind of willful insanity. The truth is the truth. Truth cannot contradict itself. It all fits together. The natural law is true and its principles are contained in Sacred Scripture. While many people reject the truth of Scripture, Christians and many non-Christians alike historically have embraced many elements of the natural law.

In her talk, "Contraception: Why Not," Dr. Janet Smith gives the following brief, yet very insightful, illustration of a fundamental component of the natural law. She explains that the natural law includes the principle that if you want things to prosper, you have to treat them in accord with the truth of their nature. If you want to grow good tomatoes, you have to treat tomato plants in accord with "tomato" nature. You have to give them nutrients, light, and water. You can't put your tomato plant in a dark closet and refuse to water it and expect it to grow good tomatoes. Similarly, if you want your old car to run, you need oil, gasoline, and a good battery. You can't put molasses in your car and expect it to run. If treated contrary to their natures, you won't get tomatoes and your car won't reach your driving destination.

Nature reveals and reason confirms the fact that human life and sexuality has its own law, or nature, and unless lives are lived in accordance with that truth and nature, blindness and chaos will result.

Healthy families more often than not give rise to happy children. If men and women do not live in accordance with the nature of sex, society will not have healthy families. It is that simple. Families form the cornerstone of any culture of society. When the gift of sex is abused—even among consenting teenagers or adults—damage is inevitable. It may take some time for the disease to really show itself, and it may not visibly infect every family equally, but eventually, breaking the natural moral law leaves a trail of disorder.

Catholic teaching on sexuality (and so much more) is not simply scripturally revealed wisdom. The fullness of moral truth is contained in the Bible, but so much of Christian moral teaching is something that human beings can discover

> **Nature reveals and reason confirms the fact that human life and sexuality has its own law, or nature, and unless lives are lived in accordance with that truth and nature, blindness and chaos will result.**

with their own reason, one of God's gifts. However, our appreciation of and ability to see the natural law is subject to our habits and environment, that is, our culture. Sadly, ours is an obscuring culture.

In the year 1932, the obscuring forces were becoming more successful in refracting the light of natural law concerning sexual behavior, but Aldous Huxley still saw the truth. The British author was an atheist when he wrote the book, *Brave New World*. Huxley wrote this novel, in part, as a response to England's embrace of contraception. His prophetic vision saw where Materialism, Consumerism, and Individualism would lead when fueled and enabled by new attitudes toward sex and family. In this dystopian novel, the future world features lots of sterile sex (engaged in from an early age), designer drugs, and babies grown in laboratories. In the world he foresees there is a near-universal separation of sex from reproduction and the family is redefined. The citizens of the Brave New World think they are happy with their abundance of casual sex, designer lives, designer drugs, and great movies; but in fact they mostly live in a disconnected, hopeless, loveless humanity. To the prophetic voices of Gandhi, Luther, Freud, and Pius XI, we now add Huxley.

Natural Law Revealed

In Christian theology, the Ten Commandments reveal, in broad strokes, the natural moral law. I think it strange that many Christians outside of Catholicism are not really interested in natural law today. What is even more bizarre is that some "Christians" reject the Ten Commandments and the whole of natural law as unnecessary under grace. (Catholicism embraces the Ten Commandments, along with the Beatitudes, as *essential, fully knowable,* and *possible to follow* in union with the Commandments of love because of God's grace.) One is saved by grace lived in faith, hope, and love. Love is to keep the Commandments; love is perfected in the Beatitudes and brings a peace and happiness the world/flesh/devil can neither give nor take away.

A beautiful application of the principles of the natural law is the Declaration of Independence, which references our "Creator" and "self-evident truths." Most unfortunately, natural law is no longer taught as the foundation stone of United States' law in our law schools. Not accidentally, the Ten Commandments are being removed from courthouses across the country, in part because there is an objective and absolute morality, including a sexual morality, assumed by natural law. We, as a nation, have given in to the lie of relativism whereby we determine our own shifting truths based on little more than convenience, precedent, popular opinion, and lust. The mantra of the "dictatorship of relativism" is the *insane* contradiction that the only absolute truth is that there *is* no absolute truth. The natural law, the Ten Commandments, and the Constitution point to the need for grace and mercy (and jails!) because we fail to keep the law. But to change the moral law (the Way) or the Truth (as if it could change) to suit our weakness is the very definition of being lost.

> **In Christian theology, the Ten Commandments reveal, in broad strokes, the natural moral law.**

12

Sacred Tradition

W hy didn't the Catholic Church change Her teachings to "keep up with the times" when so much of the rest of the world had "progressed," and there was so much pressure within the Church to change? Catholics who know their faith know that the Pope, and bishops in union with him, does not use mere human wisdom when defending and defining the moral truths of the faith. The Church, the bride of Christ, is one with Her Spouse, Jesus. *However, the Church is not the author of the Truth that She might change it.* Rather, She is the steward of the teachings entrusted to Her by God. The Church ushered in the Kingdom, but as you may know, the Kingdom on earth at present is full of both weeds and wheat (Matthew 13:24); it is like a wide net that has been cast which contains both good fish and bad (Matthew 13:47).

The Holy Spirit actively prevents the Church from teaching falsehood in matters of faith and morals. God is not restricting human freedom by preventing the Church from teaching error; He actually makes human freedom possible, for authentic human freedom requires the truth and virtue.

There is an *infallible* certainty that God will lead the Church, established by Jesus Christ and led by "Peter," to teach the truth in matters of *faith and morals*. Getting those who claim the Catholic faith to embrace, teach, and live the faith is clearly another issue. Nonetheless, the teachings of the Church have been consistent for 2,000 years and are not difficult to find. And make no mistake: This century's disordered behavior is not new; rather, it has ancient origins. There have been sex potions, prostitutes, abortions, infanticide, divorce, adultery, crude condoms, and homosexual sex from the earliest days of man's fall from grace. What is new is how widespread these behaviors have become and how they are now embraced by professed followers of Jesus Christ.

> **The Church is not the author of the Truth that She might change it. Rather, She is the steward of the teaching entrusted to Her by God.**

The authentic Christian teaching on sex, rooted in Scripture and natural law, is unchanging. However, if you read newspaper headlines you might be led to believe that the teaching is changing every few months...but those headlines are generally half-truths and sometimes outright lies, recycled every few years, purportedly changing and changing again the unchanging truth.

Authority

Jesus said to His Apostles, "As the Father sent me, so I send you" (John 20:21), "Whoever listens to you listens to me" (Luke 10:16), and "I will give you the keys of the kingdom of heaven, and whatever you bind on earth will be bound in heaven, and whatever you loose on earth will be loosed in heaven" (Mathew 16:19). God has blessed the Catholic Church with His own teaching authority in matters of faith and morals. The moral principles of the Church are not true because the Church teaches them; they are taught because they are true—there is no falsehood in them. Do not be misled by all kinds of strange, "progressive" teachings. Jesus is the same yesterday, today, forever. The attacks on the Church from within and without, including confusion about the difference between a moral teaching (defining adultery) and a discipline (e.g., abstaining from meat on Friday), do not change the fact that the Catholic Church has been given the authority to give binding moral teaching.

The moral principles of the Church are not true because the Church teaches them; they are taught because they are true.

13

For What Purpose?

Aristotle, a pre-Christian scientist and philosopher, said to even begin to determine if something is good one must determine the purpose of that thing; from purpose only can one determine if something (or someone) is truly good or perfect. What is the essential reason, that is, the purpose for sex? The Church and nature teach that sex has naturally-linked purposes: babies and bonding, infants and intimacy, children and communion. By nature these things belong together. Contraception, masturbation, pornography, sterilization, and homosexual sex unnaturally separate them. The world screeches in a voice that grows louder every day: "Sex is not about babies or the bond between husband and wife. Sex is marginally and rarely about infants or children. *The purpose* of sex is first and always (and often short-lived) emotional and physical pleasure...in our Brave New World."

To proclaim that the purpose of sex is first of all pleasure is like saying that the purpose of morphine is

From purpose only can one determine if something (or someone) is truly good or perfect.

pleasure. Drugs are meant to restore health. Drugs make one feel better. Drugs are intended to heal and/or to relieve pain... but their purpose is not escape or pleasure, even though relief may be pleasurable. The abuse of drugs makes them a poison. A friend of mine who has seen the scourge of methamphetamine in his community said to me, "I might need to try some of that meth—it must be really good stuff if in order to use it you're willing to lose your family, health, career, and neglect your kids." The damage seen in drug addicts and the families of drug addicts often takes months or years to become undeniable. The poison of the misuse of sexual activity is also a destructive force, though it may take years, even decades for the damage from this vice to become obvious as it undermines the purpose of marriage and sex. It may never reach the stage of being beyond "denial," but for those with eyes to see, we are at least nearing that point.

Your Purpose

What is the purpose of a human being? To know, love, and serve God and be happy with Him for eternity. How does a man or woman strive to fulfill his or her purpose? To obediently follow God's call and fulfill the good works God has planned for him or her.

It is fundamental to Christianity, first, that life, our bodies, marriage, and sex all have a purpose; and second, that we are each called to perfection. Love is our purpose. God, as a Potter, molds and shapes us by grace toward perfection.

Our fallen human nature, unaided by grace, tends powerfully toward a shallow selfishness. We eagerly believe half-truths when we think we will benefit, emotionally or otherwise. Without grace we are literally enslaved to sin and believing in lies. Freed by grace we are called to conform our lives to Jesus, who is the Truth.

Sterilization, masturbation, porn, and homosexual sex divorce men and women from the purpose of sex, the purpose of their bodies, the purpose of marriage, and the purpose of life. These things divorce sex from life-giving power. It is as if a

What is the purpose of a human being?

slow-acting poison is poured into a natural and healthy system of relationship, sex, life, marriage, and purpose.

Contraception treats fertility as a disease. It creates confusion about the purpose of our bodies and our lives. It has introduced sterility as good and homosexual sex as natural. The contraceptive mentality has undermined discipline and self-control (lived as fidelity or virginity), resulting in their being regarded as questionable, unnatural, unhealthy, and open to mockery and ridicule. One can imagine someone looking at Jesus laying down His life for His friends and saying, "wasted meat."

The call of our culture, the government, the women's movement, and the gay rights lobby is not to reconsider the natural law and the teaching of Scripture in the face of the collapse of the family. No, the clamor is for more, "better" contraception and the distribution of condoms at no charge to students in middle school. And it seems on the surface to make perfect sense. I know, I used to feel the same way, but it is a faulty logic based on lies.

14

The Spiritual Battle

The devil is a liar and a murderer, but he does not often tell an outright lie; rather, he prefers half-truths, sowing doubts, and appealing to our natural desires for truly good things.

We see the model of all temptations "In the beginning." The original temptation of the Garden of Eden, recorded for us in the first book of the Bible, was to believe a lie. The lie was essentially: *God is keeping something from you! Disobey and you will be like God, and know (choosing for yourself) good and evil.* The goal of this lie, and all temptations since, was for humanity to disobey and "divorce" or break communion with God. The serpent said to the woman, Eve:

> "*Did God really say,* 'You must not eat from any tree in the garden'?" The woman said to the serpent, "We may eat fruit from the trees in the garden, but God did say, 'You must not eat fruit from the tree that is in the middle of the garden, and you must not touch it, or you will die.'"
>
> "*You certainly will not die,*" the serpent said to the woman. "For God knows that when you eat from it your eyes

will be opened, and you will be like God, knowing good and evil."

When the woman saw that the fruit of the tree was *good* for food and *pleasing* to the eye, and also *desirable* for gaining *wisdom*, she took some and ate it. She also gave some to her husband, who was with her, and he ate it (Genesis 3:1-6 NIV, emphasis added).

Let's express this temptation in modern terms and, specifically, in the context of this book.

"*Did God really say...?*" In today's terms: "Look at our scientific research. Look at happy pictures of the 'modern family'; furthermore, see how numerous you people have become. *Did God really even say,* 'Be fruitful and multiply and fill the earth?' Did He really mean that? That's a myth. It's irresponsible!"

"Look, a researcher says he has found a possible biological predictor that some people are more likely to be promiscuous and unfaithful, or to experience same-sex attraction...and since God made you that way and, of course, wants you to be happy, then it must be alright! You have sexual needs, God knows you have needs. All of that self-control and patience, that doesn't make me happy. Does it make you happy? *Did God really say,* 'You are not allowed to be happy?' That is no God I want to believe in."

"*You certainly will not die!*" would be rephrased today, "Spiritual *death* is so mean and medieval; it is as though God is a bully, frightening people with 'death'. Is there really even such a thing as *deadly* sin? Who made that up? People with real faith—happy faith like *yours*—can't make a shipwreck of faith. No, you know that you are OK! You will not die. There is no hell! That is just the archaic Church, playing God, trying to keep something good from you and cling to its power, while keeping women, homosexuals, and civilization down. What is a sin anyway? Who determines what a deadly sin is? God just wants you to be happy and blessed. You will *not* die—you *have* the abundant life and no one, no One, can take it from you—you're already saved."

> # Did you know that the false gods that surrounded the Jewish people were gods of prosperity, fertility, sex, and pleasure? Those false gods are still with us.

The best Satan can offer is partial truths that appeal to our desire for truly good things such as intimacy, communion, bonding, pleasure, and freedom from distress. The appeal of sex outside of marriage and the Pill and other forms of contraception have been so powerfully embraced because they, too, can *appear* to be good, pleasing, and wise.

Did you know that the false gods—the Baals—that surrounded the Jewish people in the Old Testament were gods of prosperity, fertility, sex, and pleasure? Those false gods are still with us. They are now anonymous, or under an alias, or even masquerading as the *I'm OK, you're OK* Jesus. The "feel-good, sentimental Jesus" and "modern day golden calf-worship" prioritize professed practicality, emotionalism, money, power, and sex above the cross of Christ which, as you may recall, is the difficulty of doing the *right thing* in the face of tremendous temptation or persecution. St. Paul reminds us in his First Letter to the Corinthians: "For I resolved to know nothing while I was with you except Jesus Christ and Him crucified" (2:2).

Some Christians like to quote the Old Testament figure, Joshua, who was to lead the nation Israel into the Promised Land after Moses' death. Joshua's challenge was to settle the people Israel in the midst of nations worshipping gods that allowed for sexual excess and child sacrifice. Joshua gave the Israelites two alternatives (the false gods or the God of Israel) and then he famously said, "As for me and my household, we will serve the Lord" (Joshua 24:15). Many modern Christians quote the patriarch Joshua and use his words as their own, and then still freely embrace the gods of sexual license (pornography, fornication, contraception, and adultery—including divorce and remarriage) and child sacrifice (abortion).

Jesus said, "The thief comes only to steal and kill and destroy; I came so that they might have *life* and have it *abundantly*" (John 10:10). People really like that line of Scripture, and so do I. But what has our Lord to say about lust and divorce (with remarriage)? How does the modern world feel about our Lord's teachings on lust, serial marriages, and adultery? How well do *you* embrace the Lord's difficult teaching?

"You have heard that it was said, 'You shall not commit adultery.' But I say to you, everyone who looks at a woman with lust has already committed adultery with her in his heart" (Matthew 5:27-28).

It has been said: "If we do not strive to behave as we believe, we are doomed to believe as we behave." Striving toward maturity, toward wholeness, that is, holiness, involves embracing God's call to purity and self-control.

Jesus Came to Save!

I urge you, brothers and sisters, don't be your own god and don't substitute Baal and the golden calf for Jesus and His cross. Let Almighty God, Father and Creator of all that is visible and invisible, be God, and you a sinner in need of God's mercy! Jesus did not come to pretend sin does not exist; *He came to save sinners.* Jesus, who loves you; Jesus, who assumed your fallen nature with its penalties due to sin—suffering, alienation, and death that were nailed to the cross along with Him—came to save us all from ourselves and from the Enemy. Do not deny His gift by denying your sin or the sins of the world.

Jesus acknowledged the difficulty of this life, and He conceded that temptation and sin are bound to happen. But He also made repentance and humility an occasion of growth, "Where sin increased grace abounded all the more" (Romans 5:20). God really can bring good from bad.

A True Struggle

Consider if you will a married couple with a young child or children. The husband works out of town and they, in their struggle, give in and occasionally use contraception. They really want to trust God, live the teachings of the Church, respect the integrity of sex, and they desire to pass holiness and respect of the body on to their children by word and example; however, they have stumbled in weakness.

> **You *can* be holy!**

As this couple strives and seeks in repentance and humility to grow in self-control and trust, they may choose to welcome one or more additional children or they may sacrificially and prayerfully practice Natural Family Planning to postpone conceiving and grow in virtue. If they excuse themselves from *striving* for self-control, greater conversion, and greater trust in God, then failure and sin will take root and in time bear bad fruit, or at least prevent the fruits of the Holy Spirit from growing.

Our fallen nature always wants what appears to be the easy way out, but at times the easy way is the wrong way. True, "Self-mastery is a *long and exacting work*," and Catholic teaching acknowledges it as such. "One can never consider it acquired once and for all. It presupposes renewed effort at all stages of life" (*Catechism of the Catholic Church* 2342). But God has not commanded what He does not give the strength to do. You *can* do this! You *can* be holy!

It is absolutely critical to believe that *Jesus came to save the world rather than to condemn it*. As Jesus draws us closer, we will, by the light of His grace, see more clearly our selfishness and lack of trust in God. Only at that point can we be changed by

Him, continue our conversion, and further our ongoing return to God (repentance). The alternative is to justify ourselves and step away from Jesus, who is the Light, into darkness.

Perhaps the most critical point of this entire book is to understand and embrace the difference between excusing one's weakness and fallen nature by embracing a lie versus by grace, turning to Jesus as the Way, Truth, and Life for mercy and strength.

The gulf between "I have no sin" (and the actions and beliefs which flow from this position) and "I am a poor sinner in need of mercy" (and what flows from there) is eternal. It is the difference between Jesus being one's Rock and salvation and His being "the cornerstone rejected" and the "stumbling stone."

Lord, make me an instrument of Your peace.
Where there is hatred, let me sow love;
where there is injury, pardon;
where there is doubt, faith;
where there is despair, hope;
where there is darkness, light;
and where there is sadness, joy.

O, Divine Master,
grant that I may not so much seek
to be consoled as to console;
to be understood as to understand;
to be loved as to love;
for it is in giving that we receive;
it is in pardoning that we are pardoned;
and it is in dying that we are born to eternal life.

15

Authority, Opinions, and Conversion

S omeone once told me after a talk about a difficult subject that he "agreed with my opinion." I don't think you want my opinion. Jesus Christ, our Lord and Savior, said Himself, "My teaching is not my own but is from the one who sent me" (John 7:16). As I mentioned earlier, Jesus said to His Apostles,

- "As the Father sent me, so I send you" (John 20:21);
- "Whoever listens to you listens to me" (Luke 10:16);
- "I will give you the keys of the kingdom of heaven, and whatever you bind on earth will be bound in heaven, and whatever you loose on earth will be loosed in heaven" (Mathew 16:19).

This sending of the apostles did not die with the original Twelve. God has blessed the Church with His own teaching authority in matters of faith and morals. Of course I have "my opinions," but what this short book summarizes is a personal reflection on the objective, unchanging, clear moral teachings of Christianity.

If you have been told that Jesus Christ or Christianity or

Jesus has not left us orphaned.

the Catholic Church teaches that sex outside of marriage is *not* a serious sin that destroys grace in the soul, or that homosexual sex is a healthy expression of affection, or that homosexual marriage as a blessed union is possible, then you have been lied to. These things break the natural and scriptural laws and principles regarding sex. These things are serious sins that undermine God's grace and sow destruction in minds, hearts, and families. Contraception is a sin. Masturbation is a sin. Sexting, buying, selling, and viewing pornography are sins. These sins cause the misery and ruin of souls starting right here on earth and lead to hell.

I am a believer. I believe that Jesus came, not simply to die for us but to live in us and establish His Church, His Body, His Presence. *God did not simply give us the Scriptures and leave us to argue endlessly about its meaning.* Sadly, many Christians make an idol out of the paper and ink of their Bibles. The Bible can "say" almost anything you, or anyone, wants it to say, or it can be silent or obscure on almost any subject a particular reader or preacher chooses.

In addition to reason, natural law, and Sacred Scripture, at times humanity needs an unambiguous authority to bind and loose and to teach with authority. The world needs the one, holy, catholic, and apostolic Church. Jesus has not left us orphaned.

There is a saying, "All things are possible with God," but it has a qualifier: All things *that are possible* are possible with God. Just as a square circle is impossible, so adultery as blessed is impossible, so Christian homosexual marriage is impossible. For the Christian to "see" homosexual marriage, etc., as real and good is akin to seeing the king in Hans Christian Andersen's fable fully clothed, as he parades nakedly down the street.

Conversion/Sanctification/Repentance is a Lifelong Process

Dr. Kim A. Hardey, an OBGYN of Lafayette, Louisiana, recorded a talk about his journey from pro-abortion medical student, to anti-abortion but pro-contraception doctor, to anti-contraception personally, to refusing to prescribe contraception in his practice, to being a kind of lay evangelist spreading the true teaching of the Church concerning sex and marriage. This was a difficult upward climb involving a *series of conversions* for him. His is a powerful testimony. Throughout all the stages of his conversions, he was Catholic. Dr. Hardey had to face the sobering realities that it was a mortal sin for him to dispense drugs he knew caused abortion and that he no longer could perform tubal ligation. Dr. Hardey found it necessary to *seek out* a priest with the courage to teach and affirm him in the challenging truths of the Church's teaching.

> # There is a holy and pure perspective on life, beauty, and sex that so much of the world is simply blind to.

Contrary to much of the false gospel preached today, following Jesus is often a profound and seemingly unrelenting struggle against our tendency to fall off the wagon, throw others under the bus, and compromise the truth. Jesus said,

> "Enter through the narrow gate; for the gate is wide and the way is easy that leads to destruction, and those who enter by it are many. For the gate is narrow and the way is hard, that leads to life, and those who find it are few" (Matthew 7:13-14).

Conversion and Perseverance Can Be Hard Work

"The Kingdom of God is like treasure hidden in a field" (Matthew 13:44). Sometimes we have to sweat and struggle to uncover the treasure, but when we really find it we will sell everything to buy that field. Christianity is not a pop-psychology, quick fix, feel-good religion for wimps. However, healed by God's grace one becomes free; there is a holy and pure perspective on life, beauty, and sex that so much of the world is simply blind to. As one progresses in the spiritual life, there is purity, self-control, and joy along with the "cross," unknown and unimagined by much of the world. I have experienced this truth. I know it to be true; *I know it to be true.* It is also true that purity and self-control must be lived one day at a time.

Alcoholics Anonymous, also known as *The Big Book,* says, "Half measures availed us nothing." The true Christian teachings about sex, like few other teachings, pull back the curtain on our "half measures," our protracted adolescence, hidden lack of trust in God, lukewarm faith, selfishness, greed, and reliance on the flesh. Furthermore, the challenge to be holy and live the fullness of God's truth highlights our need for a lifetime of repentance, conversion, reconciliation, and sanctification. When people are converted to the whole truth regarding the body, sex, the sacrifice of Christ, and their personal call to follow Jesus, they can more clearly see a need for a radical reorientation of life from the stream of modern culture. In today's world, authentic discipleship necessitates swimming against the current and standing out from the crowd...like someone entering a narrow gate away from the wide road. Additionally, with each conversion,

With each conversion, the believer becomes richer in mercy.

the believer becomes richer in mercy and less likely to coldly condemn others, less likely to "throw stones."

St. Thomas Aquinas said of human beings that with our fallen natures we are born into the double darkness of sin and ignorance. Jesus is the light of the world. Jesus brings knowledge and understanding. Our nature is corrupted and our reason darkened, but we can know the truth and each of us will be held accountable and, I pray, crowned in glory for our loving response to the truth.

> I urge you therefore, brothers, by the mercies of God, to offer your bodies as a living sacrifice, holy and pleasing to God, your spiritual worship. Do not be conformed to this age but be transformed by the renewal of your mind, that you may discern what is the will of God, what is good and pleasing and perfect (Romans 12:1-2 NAB).

16

Holy Communion

Jesus established the New Covenant (marriage, if you will) in His blood and gave us Holy Communion—making us one with Him. Jesus Christ sacrificed Himself for us, "This is My Body which will be given up for you... This is the Chalice of My Blood, the Blood of the New and Eternal Covenant, which will be poured out for you..." Jesus says, "Follow me." St. Paul tells us, "You have been purchased for a price." "You are not your own." "Do not be conformed to the world." "Make of yourselves a living sacrifice."

The Good News is that at the end of the day, we do not want to be our own; we want to belong, and not belong superficially but deeply, intimately, personally, permanently, in truth. There was in Greek mythology the idea that the god Zeus divides individual "human beings" from a single whole into two separate beings, and that each "half" spends life looking for the other, seeking wholeness. This story exemplifies the innate knowledge, experience, and understanding that we human beings have of our need

> # Nobody has to teach us that we want to be in communion with Eternal Love.

for communion. Nobody has to teach us that we want to be in communion with Eternal Love, and nobody has to teach us what love is, but our hearts do have to be open to these truths.

Jesus' self-sacrifice and the giving of His Body and Blood in obedience for His bride, the Church, is the centerpiece of Catholic worship. It is both a lived example and a call to imitate. In the Eucharist, we are invited to "do this in memory" of Jesus, and the one timeless and eternal act of love given by Jesus for His bride, the Church, is made present. Through a humble and pure participation in the Eucharist, we "remember," we renew the New Covenant (our marriage with God, our adoption into God's family), and we strengthen our communion with Jesus, crucified, risen, and glorified. We are called into a deeper supernatural bond with God.

To the Romans

If a person tenaciously embraces something false, a misunderstanding or misperception, as the "truth," then this "truth" becomes offensive. In light of this book, please note what St. Paul wrote in his letter to the people of ancient Rome. I hope you can see that he is describing not just ancient Rome, but modern America, and that it likely applies equally to each generation of the human family.

Ever since the creation of the world his [God's] invisible nature, namely, his eternal power and deity, has been clearly perceived in the things that have been made. So they are without excuse; for although they knew God they did not honor him as God or give thanks to him, but they became futile in their thinking and their senseless minds were darkened. Claiming to be wise, they became fools, and exchanged the glory of the immortal God for images resembling mortal man or birds or animals or reptiles.

Therefore God gave them up in the lusts of their hearts to impurity, to the dishonoring of their bodies among themselves, because they exchanged the truth about God for a lie and worshiped and served the creature rather than the Creator, who is blessed forever! Amen.
For this reason God gave them up to dishonorable passions. Their women exchanged natural relations for unnatural, and the men likewise gave up natural relations with women and were consumed with passion for one another, men committing shameless acts with men and receiving in their own persons the due penalty for their error.

And since they did not see fit to acknowledge God, God gave them up to a base mind and to improper conduct. They were filled with all manner of wickedness, evil, covetousness, malice. Full of envy, murder, strife, deceit, malignity, they are gossips, slanderers, haters of God, insolent, haughty, boastful, inventors of evil, disobedient to parents, foolish, faithless, heartless, ruthless. Though they know God's decree that those who do such things deserve to die, they not only do them but approve those who practice them (Romans 1:20-32).

So Now What?

Ask, seek, knock, strive after the fullness of truth and then believe it and live it. If this book has helped you reconsider your beliefs about sex, great, but it would be much better if it helped you change your behavior. It has been demonstrated over and over that our actions contribute as much or more to our beliefs as our beliefs do to our actions. Live a disciplined life and you will believe and understand that life more clearly. Live the lie and the lie will become your gospel.

> **It has been demonstrated over and over that our actions contribute as much or more to our beliefs as our beliefs do to our actions.**

Epilogue

The Future

John Wesley once said, *"What one generation tolerates the next will embrace."*

Contraception was the seed; abortion, sexual chaos, and the coming persecution are the worst of the fruit. As uncomfortable for some as it may be, I have to draw the line even more boldly from contraception and intentional sterilization to a societal embrace of mandatory contraception and homosexual sex and the coming persecution of anyone who believes in natural law.

> **"What one generation tolerates the next will embrace."**
> ~ **John Wesley**

The Progression of Cultural Change

1930s—An overwhelming rejection of contraception, abortion, divorce, cohabitation, homosexual sex; homosexual marriage was unheard of...something like a square circle.

1960s—Rapidly growing and now general acceptance of contraception but a general rejection of cohabitation, homosexual sex, divorce and remarriage.

1970s—Abortion legalized nationally; nearly universal acceptance of contraception; divorce increasing; cohabitation rising; "open" marriages becoming more common; homosexual sex still "illegal" in many cities, states, and the military, but homosexual subculture gaining acceptance.

1980s—Homosexuality "coming out of the closest"; AIDS epidemic draws attention and some sympathy toward promiscuous homosexual sex; divorce has peaked; cohabitation is commonplace; teen pregnancy is exploding; families begin collapse, abortion is taken for granted.

1990s—"Don't ask/don't tell policy" allows closeted homosexuals to serve in the military; gay pride is on parade in the public square like never before; cohabitation is "in" while marriage is becoming less the norm; oral sex is declared "not sex" by the U.S. President; partial-birth abortions are legal; test-tube conceptions and in-vitro pregnancy with "selective reduction" are commonplace.

2000-2008—Those extra "reduced" living and dead embryos have become available for experimentation and exploitation (you were once an embryo, an unborn child). These experiments on living and dead "embryos" are accepted as good stewardship of a resource. Homosexuality is going mainstream, civil unions are accepted, same-sex marriage is being called for.

2008-2014—U.S. President endorses homosexual sex; gay sex is okay in the military; infanticide is practiced (unwanted children "accidentally" born alive should be left to die); homosexual "marriage" growing; adoption agencies shut down for failure to give children to homosexual parents; Plan B (abortion pill) given out to middle school children (but not aspirin). California and New Jersey make it illegal to tell an adolescent that homosexual attraction is a disordered sexual appetite, the genesis of which is unknown, but may be more or less lasting depending on one's actions and environment. Laws have been passed requiring employers (against their will and religious convictions) to provide contraception and "medicines" that cause abortion.

2014-2020—Publicly proclaiming and teaching the historical and eternal Christian truth about life, marriage, and the place and purpose of sex will be proclaimed as illegal in places as a hate crime, or considered bullying or (painfully ironic) intolerance.

Persecution is Coming

Another prophecy of Pope Paul VI in *Humanae Vitae* was that governments, forgetful of Divine and natural law, would impose contraception and abortion on the citizens who don't know what is really true or good.

Voltaire said, "It is dangerous to be right when the government is wrong." John the Baptist had his head chopped off because he spoke out against an unlawful marriage. St. Paul said of certain people in his day, "Their god is their belly; and their glory is in their shame; their minds are set on earthly things" (Philippians 3:19). Here the belly represents all the appetites of the flesh—food, drink, sex, etc. In another place, St. Paul tells the people of ancient Greece that sexual sin is a form of idolatry (worshiping a false god). Today, sexual immorality is still a form of idolatry, and there will be a "religious persecution" against "infidels" who do not worship or refuse to approve the worship of the idol. Moreover, this persecution will be carried out by misguided governments using the laws of relative morality and the "might makes right" of nations gone mad.

> # "It is dangerous to be right when the government is wrong."
> ## -Voltaire

The golden calf of America is as it was in the desert between Egypt and the Promised Land: the god of money, sex, and power. But today, the god of sex is gorging on lust, artificial sterility, and homosexual sex. The centerpiece of worship is (unborn) child sacrifice. The earth is our second god. These two gods give rise to the imperial dogma of population control. Blasphemy and/or failure to worship these gods will be punished.

The failure to worship the gods of a culture all too often ends badly for the non-believer. This, too, is part of our fallen nature; we really do have a tendency to throw others under the bus...or fine them, increase their taxes, demand their silence, or arrest them for hate crimes. If one looks, it is not hard to see the religious enthusiasm for environmental activism, contraception, and killing babies. There is a kind of evangelical fervor among some to promote homosexual marriage as true justice for all and paint those against it as hateful (sinners). If one looks with eyes to see, these movements have their commandments and sins, their evangelists, processions, flags, parades, altars, sacrifices, hymns, and soon to come...inquisitions.

Our response to persecution must be a personal and deepening conversion and love, even of our enemies. Remember that our Lord was crucified for telling the truth,

110

and love tells the truth, in kindness and charity, even when the truth brings persecution. If your love for Jesus is not something you want to share with others—you do not know what it means to love Jesus.

This world is not the eternal city. It is not home. The Christian is a pilgrim away from home. Our destiny is not to make this a more eco-friendly planet on which to die an eternal death. We are here to know, love, and serve God. The more we do that, the more clearly Christ will live in us, and the more clearly our lives will mirror His. The more our lives mirror His, the more blessed we will be. For then we will be overcoming our fallen nature and living our true nature in the image and likeness of God. Jesus said:

> "Blessed are the poor in spirit, for theirs is the kingdom of heaven.
> Blessed are those who mourn, for they shall be comforted.
> Blessed are the meek, for they shall inherit the earth.
> Blessed are those who hunger and thirst for righteousness, for they shall be satisfied.
> Blessed are the merciful, for they shall obtain mercy.
> Blessed are the pure in heart, for they shall see God.
> Blessed are the peacemakers, for they shall be called sons of God.
> Blessed are those who are persecuted for righteousness' sake, for theirs is the kingdom of heaven.
> Blessed are you when men revile you and persecute you and utter all kinds of evil against you falsely on my account. Rejoice and be glad, for your reward is great in heaven, for so men persecuted the prophets who were before you" (Matthew 5:3-12).

We either strive to behave as we believe or we will be doomed to believe as we behave.

SEX, LIES, AND YOUR FUTURE

Acknowledgements

"There is nothing new under the sun" (Ecclesiastes 1:9). I do not claim any of this book to be original; rather, it is my effort to consolidate and personalize the Christian teachings on sex and the pursuit of happiness. My first inspiration was Dr. Janet Smith's lecture, "Contraception, Why Not," which I drew from in both categories and quotes. I decided to write and record my own talk, similar to hers, based on the timeless wisdom of the Church. That talk became the beginning of this short book.

Time was spent reading and reflecting on St. Pope John Paul II's, *Theology of the Body* and the encyclical letters, *Casti Connubii* and *Humanae Vitae*. I was also inspired by the books and talks of Christopher West written to expound on the *Theology of the Body*. The beautiful conversion story and instruction by Dr. Kim A. Hardey, *An ObGyn Talks Straight to Priests About Sex and Marriage*, also encouraged me to do something, as did many other talks, sermons, books, and individuals mentioned in the text.

Scripture references except where noted are from *The Revised Standard Version Catholic Edition*.

MPO

About the Author

Reverend Michael O'Connor is a native of Ocean Springs, Mississippi and the youngest of five children. He graduated from Ocean Springs High School in 1983, and from the University of Southern Mississippi in Hattiesburg in 1987, where he received his bachelor's degree in psychology. Upon graduation, Father O'Connor was commissioned into the United States Air Force as a Second Lieutenant. He served as a military officer, both on active duty and in the Mississippi Air National Guard, principally in Radar Operations, Surveillance, and Air Weapons Control. Father O'Connor attained the rank of Major and worked full-time for the Mississippi Air National Guard from 1990 until he answered the call to enter the seminary in 2000.

Father O'Connor attended Notre Dame Seminary in New Orleans, Louisiana and was ordained a priest of the Lord Jesus Christ on June 11, 2005. In 2007, he was appointed pastor of Sacred Heart Catholic Church in Dedeaux (Pass Christian, Mississippi), and in 2014 Fr. O'Connor was appointed pastor of Our Lady of the Gulf parish in Bay St. Louis, Mississippi.

In addition to parish ministry, Father O'Connor has done a number of parish missions and religious pilgrimages. He also serves as the spiritual director for the Cursillo Movement of South Mississippi, is a member of the Deacon Formation board, and is on the bishop's Presbyteral Council where he has served as Chair. Father O'Connor has run two marathons and enjoys fishing in his spare moments.

Suggested Reading & Listening

Alcoholics Anonymous The Big Book.

Catechism of the Catholic Church.

Eden, Dawn, *My Peace I Give You: Healing Sexual Wounds with the Help of the Saints.*

Eldredge, John, *Wild at Heart.*

Fisher, Simcha, *The Sinner's Guide to Natural Family Planning.*

Hardey, Kim, *An ObGyn Talks Straight to Priests About Sex and Marriage*, CD.

Huxley, Aldous, *Brave New World.*

Ignatius Catholic Study Bible.

John Paul II, Waldstein, Michael (Translator), *Man and Woman He Created Them: A Theology Of The Body.*

Kreeft, Peter, *Making Choices: Practical Wisdom for Everyday Moral Decisions.*

Lukefahr, Oscar, C.M., *The Search for Happiness.*

New American Bible Revised Edition.

Philokalia Books and John Paul II, *Theology of the Body in Simple Language.*

Pope Pius XI, *Casti Connubii* (On Christian Marriage).

Pope Paul VI, *Humanae Vitae* (On Human Life).

The Revised Standard Version Catholic Edition Bible.

Smith, Janet, *Contraception: Why Not*, CD.

Wood, Steven, *Young Men Breaking Free: 12 Steps to Sexual Purity.*

West, Christopher, *Theology of the Body for Beginners: A Basic Introduction to Pope John Paul II's Sexual Revolution, Revised Edition.*

Online Resources

POD Apostle, http://olgpastor.podbean.com/. Contains an archive of Fr. Michael O'Connor's weekly homilies and spiritual talks. Also available as an application for Apple devices. To download the app, visit http://olgpastor.podbean.com/mobile/.

Chastity.com, http://www.chastity.com.

Christopher West, ". . . educator, best-selling author, cultural commentator, and popular theologian who specializes in making the dense scholarship of the late Pope John Paul II's *Theology of the Body* accessible to a wide audience." http://www.christopherwest.com.

Couple to Couple League, ccli.org/. Offers information, teaching, and support for couples desiring to learn more about Natural Family Planning.

Dads.org, http://dads.org/.

Faith and Family, http://www.familylifecenterstore.net/.

Home Study of Natural Family Planning, http://ccli.org/productsservices/nfp-materials/home-study-course.php.

Rachel's Vineyard Ministries, http://www.rachelsvineyard.org. Provides post-abortion healing.

Theology of the Body Institute, http://www.tobinstitute,org. A non-profit, educational organization promoting the Theology of the Body at the popular level of both the Christian and the secular cultures.

Vatican, www.vatican.va.

Notes

Notes

Notes